S0-BKM-227

The Global Community

The Global Community

A Brief Introduction to International Relations

Second Edition

JAMES A. STEGENGA
Purdue University

W. ANDREW AXLINE
University of Ottawa

HARPER & ROW, PUBLISHERS, New York
Cambridge, Philadelphia, San Francisco,
London, Mexico City, São Paulo, Sydney

1817

Sponsoring Editor: John L. Michel
Project Editor: Eleanor Castellano
Designer: Michel Craig
Production Manager: Marion A. Palen
Compositor: Maryland Linotype Composition Co., Inc.
Printer and Binder: The Murray Printing Company
Art Studio: Vantage Art Inc.

**THE GLOBAL COMMUNITY: A Brief Introduction to
International Relations, Second Edition**

Copyright © 1982 by James A. Stegenga and W. Andrew Axline

All rights reserved. Printed in the United States of America. No part of
this book may be used or reproduced in any manner whatsoever without
written permission, except in the case of brief quotations embodied in
critical articles and reviews. For information address Harper & Row,
Publishers, Inc., 10 East 53d Street, New York, NY 10022.

Library of Congress Cataloging in Publication Data
Stegenga, James A.
    The global community.
    Order of authors' names reversed on t.p. of previous ed.
    Includes bibliographies and index.
    1. International relations. I. Axline, W. Andrew.
II. Title.
JX1395.S734   1982   327   81–6711
ISBN 0–06–040404–3   AACR2

Contents

Contents

Preface

As teachers of introductory courses in politics, international relations, and foreign policy, we have noticed that there seems to be a trend away from the use of long textbooks and toward the use of a collection of paperbacks on specific topics of the individual instructor's own choosing. While this kind of individually organized course is often more interesting for the student, the integrating framework and the basic concepts that the long textbook develops are sacrificed. It is then frequently difficult for the instructor (and more importantly for the student) to fit the pieces together, to relate, or to connect the various specialized paperbacks and topics in a coherent way.

We hope this book will help resolve this problem by providing a brief, coherent framework, as well as an introduction to many of the most important concepts and problems of international relations. Perhaps the instructor will wish to have the student read our entire book at the outset of the course as a foundation for exploring more deeply some of the topics we have but touched upon. Or, alternatively, the instructor might wish to have the student read a few of our pages at a time, accompanying our brief observations with collateral readings that delve in greater detail into any of the several dozen important topics we have introduced. Either way, the use of our framework ought to help the student toward better understanding how the topics that his or her instructor highlights fit into the whole scheme of politics in the global community.

We are also aware that many instructors of introductory political-science courses attempt at the outset to acquaint their students with the various aspects of the discipline. We hope this little volume will satisfy the need for just such a basic introduction to international politics and thereby help the student to understand how international politics fits into the overall scheme of political science.

There have been many changes in the decade of the 1970s since the first edition of this book was published. We have tried to consider these changes—in world affairs and in scholarship about world affairs—in preparing this revised, second edition. We have updated those particular situations examined, such as the turmoil in southern Africa or the complex relationship between the Soviet Union and the United States. We have expanded and deepened our analysis of the troubles in the underdeveloped world by drawing on the scholarship of the last decade in the field of political economy which highlights the role of transnational corporations in the global economy. And to the two great global problems we identified in the first edition—first, the uneasy East–West relationship that threatens nuclear catastrophe and, second, the agonies of the underdeveloped world—we have, in this edition, added a third great global challenge: the deterioration of the global environment.

We would like to thank Professors John Herz, Darril Hudson, John Mueller, Donald Puchala, Randolph Siverson, Vernon Van Dyke, and Eugene Wittkopf for reading various versions of the manuscript and offering many helpful suggestions.

JAMES A. STEGENGA
W. ANDREW AXLINE

The Global Community

Introduction

Reading this book may not be a pleasant experience for many students. Not, we hope, because the book will be judged obscurely or gracelessly written, but because we discuss, sometimes in quite sober terms, the world's unfortunately ample supply of problems. Most of us try to avoid as long as possible the painful task of recognizing and thinking about even our own personal problems. Most of us would rather not have to think about such unhappy global phenomena as the population explosion, the East–West conflict, or the obvious limitations of the United Nations. There is a little of the ostrich in all of us.

Moreover, each of us manifests a perfectly human tendency to try to avoid grappling with even those problems whose existence we admit. We all tend to hope they will disappear or be suddenly revealed as trivial after all, or we exhibit a childlike faith that something (divine intervention or technology, perhaps) or someone else (the politicians, maybe) will solve our problems while we engage in happier pursuits.

Unfortunately, the problems we discuss in this book are very real, quite serious, and increasingly relevant for each citizen on our really very small and in some ways shrinking planet. They are not going to disappear magically by themselves; they must be resolved, or at least managed; and to put faith in other people and their panaceas is naive, maybe even irresponsible. Large-scale, concerted efforts by informed, determined, talented people will be necessary if humanity is to solve the numerous problems—most of them of our own making—that threaten disaster.

The essential first step in the process is to develop a growing awareness of the nature and gravity of the challenges we face. If this small and sometimes gloomy book contributes to this awareness, it will have served its purpose.

It seems appropriate to insert here a brief note about the goal we will constantly discuss in this book. We shall focus on the struggle for world order—appropriately, because world order is a requisite for realizing other human aspirations. We shall argue that order is an elusive goal, one that presently escapes our best efforts and is clearly going to remain very difficult to achieve.

But at the same time we would like to suggest that even the achievement of world order would only be a small battle won in a much more ambitious cause. There is no particular virtue in order and stability for their own sake. Order, stability, and tranquility can be found in dictatorships, prisons, and tombs. Order in this world should thus be seen not as an ultimate goal but only as a penultimate instrument, perhaps a necessary stage or base for reaching other goals, yet not an end to be deemed intrinsically worthwhile. Order and stability are valuable only insofar as they permit or promote more fundamental, ultimate values, such as freedom, dignity, self-realization, justice, well-being, and happiness.

If order is seen as having intrinsic worth and is not employed as a basis for realizing these more fundamental human goals, then order itself becomes objectionable, even reprehensible. Furthermore, order can be overdone; if domestic order is so pervasive that it stifles creative diversity and competition, if a society becomes so orderly that it loses its dynamism and begins to stagnate, then again order has become clearly unfortunate, even destructive of other cherished values. If for world order we have to pay the price of tyranny or total homogenization, then perhaps the achievement of order will have been a mistake. If we can survive only under a global dictatorship, or if we can survive only by becoming gray and spiritless automatons, then perhaps our descendants will curse us for trying so hard to achieve such a miserable, half-alive state.

Achieving world order is the minimal requisite both for world survival and for the simultaneous realization of more basic values by the world's beleaguered people. But we would like to insist emphatically at this point—even at the risk of repeating ourselves—that we have no attachment to order for its own sake and would regard those who achieved world order and stopped there with the same contempt we feel toward domestic proponents of "law and order" who have little concern for really basic values like freedom, dignity, and justice.

The real task, then, is to do more than secure world order, in itself a large challenge. The real task is the eventual development of a decent life for all the world's people. Order is at best only a way station.

Chapter 1

The State in Global Politics

By choice and by necessity, the people on this planet find themselves interacting with one another. Human needs and spatial proximity have led people to form societies, in order to engage in joint undertakings. Of all the forms of social organization that now exist, by far the most important to international politics is the sovereign state.

The state has this primary importance because it is the basic unit of international society. The actions of states make up the bulk of international politics (though the activities of nongovernmental agencies like the Red Cross and of intergovernmental institutions like the United Nations are also, to a lesser extent, important). In this chapter we will examine the historical development of states and the state system, the character of the state, and the factors influencing the making of foreign-policy decisions. Finally, we will discuss the present status and future prospects of the sovereign state as the primary actor in global politics.

The Development of the State

Historically, the sovereign state can be seen as the result of an evolution of social organization involving an ever-expanding human community. From the extended family, to the clan, to the tribe, to the city-state, and finally to the contemporary sovereign state, the history of humanity has witnessed the continued expansion of human groupings. Beyond the level of the sovereign state there also exists what might be called a very loose society of states; but it is clear that the state itself presently is the primary unit of the international human community and of developed, integrated social organization. The state is the present culmination of the evolutionary expansion of society and polity.

The state has not always been such an important unit of the human race and international politics. Indeed, it is a relatively recent phenomenon, appearing after the Middle Ages; scholars often link its emergence to the Peace of Westphalia in 1648, marking the end of the religious wars. The state system did not, however, suddenly appear full blown at that time but rather had been in the process of slowly evolving over the preceding centuries.

As early societies settled down to a fixed territory and the people became cultivators rather than nomadic hunters and gatherers, the territorial element of social units began to become an important part of defining the community. The Greek city-state marked the culmination of this development, with the *polis* becoming the principal political unit, and with international relations marking the dealings between them, including the signing of treaties and the sending of diplomatic representatives. With the decline of Greek civilization and the conquest by Rome, these states were replaced by an empire.

With the end of the Roman Empire and the onset of the Dark Ages, the major part of the Western world changed from a single empire, politically unified if culturally diverse, into a series of decentralized feudal entities. Within these entities, centered around castles and towns, obedience and service were given by the serf or vassal in exchange for protection and maintenance from the lord. Apart from racial and language bonds, the only real unifying force during the feudal period was that of Christendom. As the small feudal unit of protection became less secure, it no longer could provide the basis for political organization. As the small unit was gathered into larger units, these grew unmanageable. Revolution in technological developments (especially the development of gunpowder) and changes in economic, social, and political relationships had a tremendous impact on the organization of the political unit. Over a period of centuries feudal wars raged within the units that were to become states. Eventually, strong people established effective control over the extended feudal aggregates, subduing rivals and ambitious vassals and thereby becoming national sovereigns. In 1576 Jean Bodin gave us the classic definition of sovereignty as the ultimate power to control people and events within the area of the state. From this development of the state based on territorial control and security has emerged the modern system of states as we know it.

Western political philosophy suggests that the state, with a government exercising power on behalf of its citizens, originated in a sort of social contract, as if the individual members of the society had come together and agreed to have a sovereign govern them in order to achieve a certain amount of order. In actuality, the political relationship between governed and ruler probably arose as some people gained power over others, either because they were stronger, smarter, or more numerous, or because they convinced the others that they possessed some supernatural powers. In any case, the historical result has been the emergence of a society wherein certain people exercise power in the name of the society.

The Character of the State

The sovereign state is generally defined as comprising three essential elements: clearly demarcated boundaries describing the territory of the state, a population that more or less permanently inhabits this territory, and a government that exercises ultimate power, or sovereignty, and to which the people accord permanent allegiance. The concept of the sovereign state, however, embraces meanings beyond the "essential elements" comprised, in this simple statement, both in terms of its historical genesis and in terms of its present-day reality. We will mention sovereignty, legitimacy, community, and nationalism.

It is the concept of *sovereignty* that really sets the state apart from all other social organizations. In being sovereign, the state possesses the exclusive ability to make ultimate decisions concerning the lives of each of its citizens, including the decision about whether they shall live or die. Moreover, in being sovereign, the state possesses the capability of taking ultimate action concerning any matter within its territorial confines to the exclusion of any other social organization, including other sovereign states. In these powers lies the meaning of sovereignty. No other social organization can usurp this capability to act in the ultimate case. The state is the primary political organization of our time, because only states have such capability.

In conjunction with this capacity to act in the ultimate contingency, the state has another aspect that qualifies it as the primary social organization of our time. This is *legitimacy*—the feeling on the part of the people that the government, which is acting in the name of the state and exercising the power of the state, is rightly entitled to do so. Feeling thus, the citizens are inclined to accept peaceably and as binding the decisions emanating from the authorities and institutions.

This social solidarity and deference to authority—both of

which promote peaceful change—indicate that in addition to society, which we have defined simply as the interaction of individuals within a certain physical proximity, there also exists a *community,* a commitment on the part of the individuals in the society to each other and to the institutions of the society.

Beyond these formal attributes of sovereignty and legitimacy, perhaps the most potent characteristic of the modern state system is the force of *nationalism.* This sentiment or emotion of nationhood felt by the populace of each state is based on a common historical heritage and a general belief that the state is the principal protector of key values. Nationalism has often motivated people to sacrifice their lives in the service of the state. Just as the state is the ultimate form of social organization, nationalism is the major source of the ultimate "we–they" distinction between citizens and their country on the one hand and foreigners and their countries on the other.

Interactions Among States

Politics is generally understood to mean the complex process for handling the disagreements that inevitably arise between people and groups that have different and frequently incompatible values and goals. The participants in the political process will employ techniques of persuasion, coercion, or outright violence as they try to accomplish their goals and promote their values.

But there are obvious differences between politics within the state (domestic politics) and politics among states (international politics). In domestic politics—at least in the older, established states—individuals and groups pursue their aims and solve conflicts according to the existing, reasonably effective, and generally accepted peaceful procedures and institutions within the state, whereas international politics is clearly deficient in these effective, regular procedures and institutions.

If the state is seen as the principal actor in international politics, then the actions of states which have effect beyond the borders of the state are the substance of international politics.

International politics, then, can be viewed largely as the result of the interactions of the foreign policies of the world's states.

The State as Actor: Foreign Policy

The foreign policy of a state is the outcome of a complicated process in which many factors, both within the state and beyond its borders, are influential. Among the more important determinants, or influences, in this process of making foreign policy are the international context, the state's power, domestic public opinion, powerful individuals and groups within the state, historical traditions, values and ideology, and national interest. Each of these important factors deserves analysis here.

The International Context

State actions in the foreign-policy realm are largely shaped by the international context. Many of the foreign-policy actions a state takes are responses or reactions to conditions or events abroad, over which the state has little or no control. A dangerously explosive situation, a sudden crisis that threatens the state's interests, a challenge or direct attack from a neighboring state, a request from a friendly regime to do (or not do) something—these are all the kinds of situations that develop external to the state and produce a foreign-policy response of some kind. And the pressures of time are often such that a response has to be made quickly and thus frequently on the basis of quite imperfect information.

The Power of the State

Foreign-policy actions are also strongly shaped by the distribution of world power. Quite obviously, the kind of actions a state can take is determined to a great extent by how much power it has relative to other states; there are, beyond doubt, many foreign-policy actions that small states would like to take but cannot, because of power and resource limitations. A state's power is fundamental to its role in international politics and strongly influences the nature and effectiveness of its foreign policies.

One of the problems in the study of international politics has always been that of defining and measuring state power. In the first place, the ability of a state to achieve its objectives is more accurately a function of the perception that other statesmen have of its power than of its objectively calculated power; perception is, in this respect, more important in international politics than reality. In the second place, the many factors that compose national power are not readily measurable or comparable; even such ingredients as military equipment or economic strength that are to some extent quantifiable cannot be accurately measured and compared with those of other states, because of the impossibility of obtaining satisfactory measurement scales or common denominators. And such intangible factors as public morale and the quality of leadership are even less calculable.

Although the concept of national power is most elusive, we must try to understand the various dimensions of national power, because power plays such an important role in international politics. The factors most often mentioned as elements of national power are geography, natural resources, population, financial and industrial capacity, military might, the nature of the government, national character, and national morale.

Geography is often mentioned as the first element of national power. A state occupies a certain relatively unchanging part of the globe; this geographic situation strongly affects national policy. Natural boundaries such as oceans or mountains render a state less accessible to invasion by hostile forces. A state with an extremely large land mass, or one whose climate is relatively hostile, is difficult for enemy troops to conquer. Moreover, the relative isolation or inaccessibility or size or climate of a given state will have a more or less direct influence on other elements of power; the state's ability to support its population and the nature of its economic and industrial activity, for example, will both be partly geographically determined.

Natural resources are another factor which figures importantly in the power of a state. Like geography, a nation's resources are usually relatively stable, but technological change can make a given resource into a dynamic element in the determination of national power. For example, only since the development of efficient methods for producing aluminum from bauxite has that ore become an important source of national power. The same holds true for oil and for uranium, which has been a key resource only since the development of methods for harnessing nuclear power.

Food is perhaps the most important single natural resource, since the population of any nation must eat to survive. Thus, a state that is self-sufficient or nearly so in foodstuffs will have an advantage over one that is heavily dependent on food imports. Again, the relative wealth of a state in food resources may change with rapid technological development. For example, a small, barren, ocean-bounded state may become virtually self-sufficient in food if new methods of extracting nutrition from the sea are developed. Or a state with little available land may become a flourishing garden spot if agricultural, irrigation, or climate-control technologies improve to permit greatly increased agricultural productivity.

The natural resources for industrial production are also important in determining the power of a state. *Energy sources* and the *basic raw materials* for production of steel and other metals are perhaps the prime examples of natural resources vital to industrial strength. Mobile warfare and the sophistication of weapons systems have increased the importance of these natural resources in contributing to national power. The shift of the European economy from coal to petroleum products as the primary source of energy, for example, has had important foreign-policy implications, because Europe has almost no petroleum resources; the European states must rely on outside suppliers to satisfy their petroleum needs.

But the existence of rich deposits of natural resources or a hospitable climate do not in themselves provide national power; rather it is the capability of the state to utilize the resources with which it is endowed. A crucial determinant of a state's ability to transform these raw ingredients into usable power is that state's *human capabilities;* this demographic element of national power is composed of both quantitative and qualitative components.

Quantitatively, the demographic element of national power depends on such considerations as the size and the geographical distribution of the population. A large population is probably necessary if a state is to become a major power in international politics. But there is certainly no direct correlation between the population of a nation and its rank in world power; if there were, then China, India, the Soviet Union, and the United States, in that order, would be the four most powerful nations on earth. This is clearly not the case. The large populations of China and India are at best of mixed value for their respective governments: a potential source of strength, but also a serious burden for their regimes. If it is apparent that an underpopulated state will suffer in terms of national power, it is equally obvious that a state whose population is too large for its territory, or too large to be supported by the natural resources and foodstuffs it produces, will be weaker because of its larger population. There must be a balance between the size of the population and the state's productivity. Also, if a population is concentrated in a very small portion of the national territory while other areas remain unpopulated, the state is vulnerable to military attack, hence occupies a weaker position in international politics than a state with an optimum geographical distribution of its population.

The age characteristics of the population are also important in the demographic element of national power. A state with a high percentage of elderly citizens who are not productive and who must nonetheless be supported by the population as a whole will be weaker for that reason. A state with a high percentage of very young people will similarly be at a disadvantage, but is potentially a more powerful state, because the youth could eventually become productive.

Qualitative considerations also modify simple numerical size as a measure of the demographic factor of national power. Of these qualitative considerations, certainly health and education levels are two of the most important. A healthy, skilled population is much more able to carry out the complex tasks necessary for exercising national power than an undereducated or physically weakened population of comparable size. Moreover, the health and educational levels of the population are closely linked to some of the quantitative elements of the demographic factor mentioned above. For instance, a sophisticated population that is knowledgeable in birth-control techniques may prevent over-population and thus contribute to national power. Or adequate medical skills may lower the infant mortality rate and thus provide a more vigorous, younger, more productive population. More directly, a certain technological level of expertise and a certain minimum health standard are necessary in order for the population to be able to develop and manage a modern industrial society and an effective military establishment.

Finally, in a discussion of national power we ought to mention some other elements that play a role, but seem to be less tangible than those so far discussed; among these are *national character* and *national morale*. The tenacity of a people or their will to survive under deprivation can clearly affect the power of a state. Often there seems to be a direct relationship between national character and state behavior. The British population's morale, cohesion, and determination to fight on against seemingly insurmountable odds certainly played an important part in Britain's survival during the first few years of World War II. Governmental performance also seems to bear importantly upon a state's ability to achieve its goals in international politics, though there is no conclusive evidence that one form of government, whether democratic or dictatorial, is more effective on the world stage.

The most visible manifestation of the combination of all these ingredients of power is the state's *military establishment*. Modern military strength, clearly so important an instrument of national policy, is largely based upon industrial strength and skilled leadership. And when statesmen are weighing their foreign-policy options, they must, and do, consider whether they have whatever military power might be needed to accomplish them.

Domestic Forces

Besides being strongly influenced in their decisions by considerations of capacity or feasibility, national leaders are also guided by domestic forces and factors as they make their choices about which foreign-policy actions to take to meet constant challenges. In today's sovereign state the principal foreign-policy decisions are made by the head of the government, that is, by the president or prime minister or dictator. That person is, in turn, influenced by other participants in the decision-making process, including the key foreign-ministry officials, military officers, intelligence specialists, political-party officials, industrial managers, and the subordinate bureaucrats in related agencies and institutions who provide information and ultimately have an important role in implementing policies. In the Western democracies, these leaders are joined in the decision-making elite by legislators, lobbyists, influential private citizens from the ranks of business or the press or the universities, and ultimately the average citizens who make their preferences known through the ballot box, pressure-group activity, public-opinion polls, and other more or less influential channels.

These participants in the complex political process of all states provide differing, often clashing, information, perspectives, and advice to the head of government, who is thus pressured by at least several factions, each of which vigorously advocates a favorite policy option. It is the decision maker's task to weigh these options and select from among them.

History and Tradition

All of these more or less influential participants in the policy process, including the head of government, will in turn be motivated and influenced by three major kinds of factors. First, the state's history has a strong bearing on any current policy choices. A state that has a long and rather consistent history of responding in a particular way to a particular kind of situation may be likely to respond that way again today and tomorrow. China has had a long tradition of behaving almost as xenophobically as it is behaving today, for example. The United States has traditionally acted self-righteously. Russia has always been secretive and suspicious. Other examples will come to mind. These historical patterns of behavior, these habits, these precedents are potent influences on decision making, if for no other reason than that a state's leaders are so largely a product of their schooling, wherein their state's historical actions are nearly always taught as having been necessary, wise, and just.

Values and Ideologies

Second, the prevailing ideology (or belief system or national creed or value structure) is sometimes a very important determinant in the foreign-policy process. Communism is an obvious example of an ideology or value structure that influences the behavior of the leaders in certain countries. But most other states have a prevailing and influential belief system, though most are neither as explicit as communism nor perhaps as potent an influence. Scholars write persuasively, for example, about the influence on United States policy of puritanism, with its strong emphasis on individual responsibility, self-righteous intolerance, and missionary zeal. Whatever the exact nature of the belief system or national creed, it is fair to say that this collection of values that is inculcated early in future statesmen by their public schools and other experiences is an important determinant in the decision process. We will touch on this matter again in Chapter 4, when we discuss the roles that attitudes, values, and moral teachings play in limiting conflict.

The National Interest

Third, and perhaps most important, a general concern for the safety and well-being of their respective nations strongly influences these participants of the policy process to try to calculate rationally which among the alternative policies suggested is the best way to achieve the state's objectives that are, in turn, at least in part rationally designed to promote the national interest. Thus, although policy makers are to some extent imprisoned by history, habits, ideologies, bureaucracies, and public opinion, they still retain some ability to calculate the relative merits, drawbacks, costs, and risks of alternative policy suggestions. And their concern for the national interest, buttressed by their obligations, will drive them to try to find the most prudent action possible.

Thus, every policy action a state takes is partially shaped by each of these many factors that has a different strength in each unique case. At times, the international context or power distribution may be quite controlling, leaving the statesman little room or time to maneuver. Sometimes, though, the international context is not so important an influence as domestic public opinion, historical tradition, or ideological fervor. Occasionally, the decisions will be quite rationally and dispassionately made by well-informed and well-advised sober statesmen, influenced by their own mental processes and intuitive judgments. There is no simple answer to the question of why states do what they do in the international arena. The only general answer we can give is to insist that the answer to the question is bound to be complex and different each time. The decisions are shaped by a host of influences that operate in a different combination in each situation.

The Future of the State

In arguing that international politics can be largely understood as the interactions of the foreign policies of more than 160 states, we assume that the sovereign state is now and will remain for the foreseeable future the paramount actor on the world stage. But, in fact, some scholars have suggested that the era of the sovereign state as we have known it since the seventeenth century may be drawing to an end. Scholars have persuasively argued, first, that technology has made it impossible for sovereign states to be as independent of each other as they were previously, and, second, that the state can no longer fulfill its major function of protecting its citizens and may, therefore, eventually disappear.

These writers emphasize the tremendous impact that rapid changes in technology have had on the social relations of the human race, particularly in international politics in modern times. They argue that the role of the sovereign state in international politics has declined, perhaps even to the point of obsolescence, because of twentieth-century developments in communications, transportation, and weapons technology. They see the results in what Andrew Scott calls "informal penetration," the ability of one state to have access to the population of another state, thus bypassing and subverting the traditional intergovernmental relationship. And another writer, John Herz, argues that the traditional major function of the state, that of protecting its population from outside harm, has been undercut by new weapons of mass destruction against which no defense is possible.

Dramatic changes in communications and transportation technology have made informal penetration possible and even inevitable as people are almost daily exposed to foreign viewpoints. Recently developed political ideologies and belief systems—democracy, socialism, pan-Arabism, communism, and others—cut across national boundaries with their strong appeals for groups within different states. The economic aid that wealthy states have given to the world's underdeveloped countries has given the donor nations a certain amount of access to the people in the recipient countries. Moreover, the technological revolution in weaponry has made large-scale military conflict a much less attractive foreign-policy option, thus promoting alternative techniques of competition, including informal penetration.

The nature of informal penetration itself is a sort of reaching inside the borders of another state to affect the population directly in one manner or other. Scott defines this process as existing "when one country's agents or instruments come into contact with the people or processes of another country in an effort to achieve certain objectives." The classic examples of informal penetration are "Trojan-horse" and "fifth-column" movements, terms for the operation of the agents of one state within the boundaries of another.

The informal access may be undertaken by agents of governmental organizations, such as the United States' International Communications Agency; or by quasi-governmental organizations, such as governmental trade organizations; or through totally nonofficial contacts: missionaries, tourists, students, teachers, and businesspeople. Through these agents, the penetrating country can influence the policy of the target nation and carry out international politics in a nonformal manner.

According to Herz, the basis of national sovereignty was the state's ability to protect its citizens against foreign attack, to provide what he calls "impermeability" or "impenetrability," to maintain the state's "hard shell." Herz argues that, historically, any unit that was able to successfully provide protection and security to human beings became the basic political unit, because people have naturally recognized whatever authority possessed the power to protect them.

The history of the development of the territorial state is marked by the ever-increasing size of the protective unit. As each unit was rendered obsolete by technology, a larger, less vulnerable unit came to take its place. Herz argues that just as the development of gunpowder rendered obsolete the walled city as a unit of protection, recent developments in weapons technology have finally and fatally undermined the territorial basis of the modern state.

The alleged obsolescence of the modern state is not the result of a single technological breakthrough that has suddenly taken place, but rather is a culmination of a series of developments that began in the nineteenth century. The Industrial Revolution, which made states economically dependent on imports, allowed economic blockade to become an effective instrument of warfare. Although blockades alone have never been sufficient to assure victory in warfare, their development weakened the impenetrability of the hard shell of the state. Psychological warfare, the use of propaganda, and the accessibility of foreign populations to subversive international ideologies further penetrated the hard shell of the state. Finally, the developments of air warfare and nuclear weapons have dealt the ultimate blow to the ability of the sovereign state to fulfill its fundamental function of protecting its population. Although the advent of aerial warfare was a revolutionary development, it was not until nuclear weapons and intercontinental-ballistic-missile delivery systems became available that the whole territorial basis of the state was eroded. With these technological advances, states become capable of rendering enemy populations completely indefensible. Now that power can destroy power from center to center, the very future of the sovereign state itself comes into question. If no state can any longer really protect its citizens, Herz suggests, perhaps the sovereign state will disappear just as did the castle with its moat and drawbridges three or four centuries ago when its hard shell became so vulnerable.

It can be seen that the forces that have brought about this rupture in the impenetrability of the state are much the same developments that have, in Andrew Scott's terms, underlain the informal penetration that has marked foreign policy; indeed, it could be argued that Herz and Scott are simply emphasizing different aspects of the effect of modern technology on international politics. Although it is clear that the sovereign state is still the primary unit of interaction in international politics, it is equally clear that the role of the state in international politics is under strong attack.

With ever-increasing contacts across national borders among private individuals, organizations, and subunits of states, it has become apparent that a full understanding of international politics requires an understanding of these transnational relations and the interdependent network of interactions which they constitute. Thus, the weakening of the role of the state as the sole actor in international relations as evoked by Herz and Scott means that the level of analysis of the international system composed of states as components must be complemented by the inclusion of these transnational actors and relations to comprehend fully the richness and complexity of contemporary international politics.

It would be premature to toll the death of the sovereign state, however. First, though the hard shells of all states have been weakened, only a few states possess the ultimate capability to completely destroy other states. And nationalistic fervor is at an all-time peak in certain parts of the world; the awful nature of modern weapons has apparently not yet alarmed the world's peoples enough to cause them to overcome their emotional attachment to the state and look elsewhere for protection. Finally, states have come increasingly to serve the economic and social welfare of their citizens, thus perhaps compensating somewhat in the popular mind for the state's reduced ability to protect its citizens. At any rate, while sovereign states might be obsolescent, they are not yet obsolete. Despite their obvious and serious weaknesses, they still show no signs of disappearing from the world arena.

But, clearly, to understand international politics in an age when the sovereign state is undergoing such important changes, some attention must be paid to the structure of the larger global community. International politics must be looked at from the point of view of the entire international system. We turn now to this analytic task.

SUGGESTED READINGS

Allison, Graham. *Essence of Decision: Explaining the Cuban Missile Crisis.* Boston: Little, Brown, 1972.

Herz, John. *International Politics in the Atomic Age.* New York: Columbia University Press, 1959.

Janis, Irving L. *Victims of Groupthink.* Boston: Houghton Mifflin, 1972.

Morgenthau, Hans J. *Politics Among Nations.* 5th ed. New York: Knopf, 1973.

Scott, Andrew M. *The Revolution in Statecraft.* New York: Random House, 1965.

Chapter 2
The International System

Whereas the sovereign state was the unit of society around which discussion was focused in the preceding chapter, the larger international society is the focal point of this short chapter. The term *international system* denotes the ensemble of all the activities that make up international relations, that is, the interactions of sovereign governments and other actors in the global community.

The Political Process

It will be helpful to examine the different ways in which conflicts are handled in the political processes in domestic and international politics by contrasting the institutions and processes of the usual domestic system of politics with the politics of the international system.

At both the domestic and international levels, politics is marked by the existence of conflicts. The state itself is the institution that has been developed to resolve conflicts within the domestic system; but as yet the international system does not have a structure that is comparable to that of the sovereign state.

Often the conflicts that arise in any society are between certain groups of the society who wish to uphold the existing status and other groups desiring social change. Such change is desirable, as well as inevitable, in both domestic and international societies. The main challenge, it would seem, is to effect social change without violence, and without the destruction of the system itself.

Generally, there are three requirements for attaining peaceful social change. First, advocates of change must be able to make themselves effectively heard and understood. To do so, they need to articulate a rather specific and limited set of objectives that a sufficiently large group of individuals can agree to present as its program for change. Second, the social and political institutions of the society must be able to absorb the pressures of change; these institutions must be flexible and responsive to constantly changing circumstances. Third and finally, the system as a whole must be able to infuse the new status with legitimacy, so that any new policy has a reasonable probability of being obeyed and enforced. These three crucially important requisites of an effective, orderly political process are generally satisfied in most of the world's domestic political systems, but are at best only partially satisfied in the international system of politics.

The political system of the United States provides a useful contrast to the international system. We are all familiar with U.S. institutional form and functioning, and would agree that the United States is a relatively integrated sovereign state within which it is possible to achieve a good deal of peaceful social change. However, it is clear from past American history and from the most recent headlines that even this fairly advanced sovereign state is not completely free from the hallmark of international politics: disorder and even civil war.

In the U.S. political system, individual differences in values and goals are quite freely expressed, and there are highly developed interest groups which articulate these attitudes in a cogent form and present them to the society for consideration and discussion. Some of these groups, such as labor unions, speak for a whole sector of society. Through such organizations the advocates of change (or of the existing status) are able to pool their individual interests into a few clearly articulated and competing points of view. Through individual contact, lobbying, the communications media, advertising, and other means, these advocates are able to make themselves effectively heard.

Even beyond these groups there is a political party system which allows separate interests expressed by various groups to be further combined, or aggregated, into several broad programs, which can compete against each other. This aggregative function that is fulfilled by the political parties provides the means for channeling public pressures in the American domestic political system.

It is the adequacy and legitimacy of the political institutions, however, that provide the keys to *successful* and *peaceful* social change. In the U.S. political system there is a highly sophisticated set of governmental institutions: legislative, executive, and judicial organs which can accommodate competing attitudes and programs. Once the political parties have performed their function of reducing the number of alternatives to a very few, the duly selected political authorities can choose the particular positions they favor and put them into effect through the passage of laws which will be administered and enforced by the executive and judicial organs.

Once a decision has been taken to follow a certain program of action, the members of the society, including those who originally held an opposing view, normally support it, or at least accept it grudgingly; the policy is thus infused with the legitimacy of the society. This legitimacy is achieved by a general feeling by the members of the society that the central institutions of the society have the right to make the decisions in the manner prescribed by the political process; in other words, there is general commitment to the procedures according to which decisions will be made and through which conflicts will be resolved in the social setting. Moreover, when there is a lack of compliance with a decision of the political system, the state has the means to achieve compliance through the exercise or threat of coercive force. In this manner an effective domestic political system is able to reconcile those inevitable differences in the values and aims of the many individuals in the society, at least to the degree that there is seldom physical violence in the resolution of political conflict.

Domestic Politics and International Politics

Since differences in values and aims, such as those we have just discussed, exist in the international society as well as in domestic society, political conflict is just as inevitable in this larger arena. The occurrence of war as a "natural" phenomenon in international politics is only one indication of the lack of accepted procedures and institutions so far developed for resolving competitions peaceably in international politics.

The political differences that exist in international society cannot always be as clearly and effectively communicated as similar differences within the sovereign state may be. States can express their particular interests in the form of foreign-policy statements, and in this behavior they are comparable to interest groups in national societies in representing diverse points of view and expressing them as specific demands. We have referred to these demands as foreign-policy objectives in our discussion of the state as an actor in international politics.

A principal deficiency in the capacity of the international

system to resolve political conflict should be readily apparent. In the international system there is no effective organization or institution that is able to coalesce the divergent foreign-policy aims of several states into broadly formulated alternative policies from which to choose a single policy outcome. There are certain groups of states which have organized their joint interests in a fairly broad area of activity, but in no case is the aggregative ability of this type of coalition so effective as is the political party in domestic political systems. Various coalitions and alliances may exist for relatively long periods of time when separate states can work together for common goals in international politics. Also, the large amount of "bloc voting" which has been seen in the United Nations suggests that a certain overlapping of interests exists among states. In fact, it could be argued that in the early cold-war period following World War II, the international system saw a rather clear dichotomization of objectives between the Soviet Union and her allies on the one hand and the United States and her allies on the other. Since then, a less dichotomized state of affairs has emerged. Now the Third World of independent nations presents an additional point of view and the Chinese brand of communism provides still another.

Even if today's ideologically split world were able to produce a choice of two or three alternatives to vie for predominance, it is clear that there are no institutions in international politics to enable one of these points of view to prevail peacefully over the others. In the usual domestic political system, the legislative body or the party/military elite constitutes an organizational apparatus for authoritatively choosing between alternative proposals. In this apparatus a decision is reached which usually contains parts of several points of view. This decision is then determined to be final, at least until the question is reopened through accepted processes. In the international system, on the other hand, the United Nations provides only the skeletal framework of a legislative body in which decisions of this nature can be made only cautiously if at all. The organization does not provide, and there is yet no international institution which can provide, the means to choose authoritatively among international policy alternatives. There simply is no international legislative body.

This lack of any institutionalized means of revising the existing status is the most important obstacle preventing the political process from resolving conflict without violence. Many conflicts go unresolved; some others are resolved by resort to force, thus revealing the relatively anarchic nature of international politics.

The absence of any institution in the international system for accommodating conflicting interests without violence is by no means the system's only shortcoming. Even if less violent forms of power were able to resolve international political conflict through an authoritative rule, there would still exist the problems of adjudicating, or resolving conflicting interpretations of the rule, and of enforcing the rules when they were violated. In the domestic political system the courts provide the means to adjudicate disputes under established law, and there is a powerful police force that enforces these rules.

The problem in the international system is not so much the lack of organs to perform these functions of adjudication and enforcement, but the decentralization of this performance, with each state acting individually to judge and to enforce its own case. There is no world court with compulsory jurisdiction to rule authoritatively on disputes; and there is nothing approaching a world police force to enforce international law and court rulings. Under international law, a single state or a group of states may decide that another state or group of states has violated international law, and may impose sanctions, including force, on the accused group. However, that this sort of action by the individual members of the international community can and does occur symbolizes precisely the quasi-anarchic nature of the international system. War is a means for one state to punish or coerce another through violent attack; and frequent resort to war as a means of settling political disputes is a primary shortcoming of the international system.

It should by now be clear that, because of its decentralization, the international system is able to perform conciliatory political functions imperfectly at best. The domestic political system is characterized by the presence of sovereignty, the centralized power to enforce the rules of the society on all the citizens. In contrast, the individual actors in the international system, the sovereign states, are subject to no higher international sovereign that can impose its will upon them.

The ability of the state to maintain order within its domestic political system, however, entails more than just its superior capacity to wield force. There is a certain commitment on the part of the citizens of an integrated state to the common heritage, to the institutions they have created for carrying out political processes, and to the society as a whole. And for the most part, the people generally believe they should obey the decisions of these institutions, even if these decisions conflict with their own personal desires. This general acceptance of the legitimacy of state actions results in a minimum amount of violence being exercised by one individual member of the society against another, and it also means that the actual coercive power of the state need be exercised only in relatively few cases. Compliance with the rules usually is widely gained without the use of sanctions.

This feeling of legitimacy is not present in the international system, and the processes that help foster this commitment at the domestic level do not operate on the international level. From the time we are small children the process of socialization works to inculcate values that create a bond of social solidarity among us, and a bond of allegiance to our governmental institutions. At the present time, these allegiances and loyalties are directed to groupings no larger than the sovereign state. National symbols such as the flag and the national anthem are revered and respected, but the international symbols of commitment and loyalty to the global community are not. It would therefore be impossible for an institution of the international system, even if it had the power to impose its will on the entire world, to carry out successful resolution of political conflict over an extended period of time. One half of the necessary elements would be present—effective coercive force. The other half would be absent—the effective legitimacy comprising the loyalty of the individuals of the global community to international institutions.

This latter element must be present for the international system to be an effective political system. In its absence, the members of the international society would not address their demands to international institutions and there would be no deference to any international decision-making institutions. There would be little likelihood of a commitment to obey the decisions of the existing institutions of the international system. It is clear, then, that an effective international political system will not be developed simply by imposing political institutions on the present, decentralized international system; rather, fundamental changes must take place at the lowest level of the political system—that is, in the attitudes and allegiances of the individual people of the world.

This extended analogy between the domestic and international system should serve to illustrate the nature of the international system of politics. Through this comparison, the basic difference between the nature of the domestic and international systems of politics can be observed. But, although the major distinction between the domestic and international systems is the degree of unauthorized use of violence, the international system has proved capable of avoiding total anarchy and of resolving or at least managing many, if not most, political conflicts. Indeed, the international system's capacity to absorb and regulate potential disruptive inputs through its own non-institutionalized mechanisms and procedures is probably its single most important characteristic. Without this capability, it could not even be considered a system in the formal sense.

On the other hand, it should be clear to anyone who reads the newspapers that just as international politics often takes place in peaceful ways, so does domestic politics sometimes involve violence. Indeed, if one looks beyond the modern industrialized societies, and sometimes if one looks within them, it can be seen that by no means do domestic politics operate so successfully as to totally eliminate violent resolution of conflict. A clear distinction can be made, however, between the *expected* and *accepted* modes of conflict resolution in the two contexts. In international politics resort to war is an often used and legitimate recourse under certain conditions, the determination of which is left to the individual states. In domestic politics resort to violence is not accepted as a legitimate recourse except under very extraordinary conditions, the determination of which is left to the central authority of the society.

Modern International Politics

Earlier we defined the international system as being the ensemble of all the interactions of the states in the world. But to describe a system requires that the kinds of interactions that take place among the units be specified.

Morton Kaplan, a scholar of international relations who is well known for his discussions of international systems, has set forth the criteria for several systems of international politics, some of which have historical counterparts, some of which do not. One of the most salient characteristics which describe international systems is the way in which the various states relate to one another. From these basic characteristics we are able to differentiate among different kinds of international systems.

The two types of international systems most frequently discussed are the balance-of-power system and the bipolar system. The distribution of power and changes in this distribution play essential roles in defining the nature of these two types of systems.

Historically, eighteenth- and nineteenth-century international relations, primarily in Europe, provide the example of the operation of the balance-of-power system. During this time the major powers of the system implemented policies likely to preserve a roughly equal distribution of power among the principal states of the system. The primary mechanism through which this was achieved was the alliance. In the balance-of-power system, large-scale outbreaks of violence were avoided through the maintenance of roughly equal states or groups of states which allied themselves in order to prevent the attempt on the part of any one state to become so powerful that it threatened to dominate the entire international system.

This type of international system relied on violence and the threat of violence inasmuch as states would resort to war in order to prevent any one state from dominating the system; but it maintained order in the sense that violence was limited and states were usually not totally destroyed. After a war, a defeated state was reinstated as an integral part of the system in order to maintain the balancing mechanism. It was necessary that the states not be divided by incompatible ideologies which would prevent the possibility of one state being the potential ally of any other state in order to offset a threatened disturbance of the power equilibrium. Alliances had to be temporary and flexible in order to maintain a certain stability in the system. The balance of power is generally credited with having provided a certain degree of stability and peace in eighteenth- and nineteenth-century international politics.

After World War II, the power distribution among the states of the world was radically different. The United States and the Soviet Union emerged as superpowers in the sense that their strengths overshadowed those of any other states in the international system. This overshadowing strength was a result of the destruction in Europe during the war, coupled with the simultaneous economic, political, and military advancement of these two superpowers. By the early 1950s the Soviet Union and the United States were not only the two greatest industrial powers the world had ever seen, but also the possessors of nearly all the world's nuclear weapons.

The bipolarity in the distribution of economic and military power between the two superpowers was reinforced and exaggerated by the great ideological rift between Soviet revolutionary communism and United States-led anticommunism which pitted the two great states in an almost religious struggle. The desire by each to expand its influence abroad led to a further bipolarization of the international system as each superpower attempted to create a large bloc of satellites, client states, and protectorates.

The bipolar international system has been basically peaceful, since the decision on the part of one of the major protagonists to resort to its nuclear weapons would clearly threaten civilization itself. This peace is a result of deterrence, or the balance of terror, in which each superpower, while capable of completely destroying the enemy, remains vulnerable to complete destruction itself. As is the case with the balance-of-power system, not all violence is ruled out; but violence that might destroy the system itself is in fact excluded as an instrument of national policy. Thus, a relative stability, albeit a frightening one, is maintained.

Both the balance-of-power international system and the bipolar international system provide a certain stability and limitation on the use of violence in international politics. Within both of these systems, the decentralization of power (in the hands of numerous militarily significant governments), rather than the centralized control of force, allows international relations to proceed without degenerating into a perpetual state of anarchy and war. The distribution of power within the system limits the incidence and intensity of coercive force, while the political processes which resolve conflict function in a relatively noninstitutionalized and decentralized manner as compared to those in the domestic political system.

In summary, the processes of the international system of politics can profitably be compared to and contrasted with the processes of the domestic political system, each resolving conflicts in its own way with a greater or lesser degree of actual violence. At both "levels" problems and conflicts arise; at both levels procedures and mechanisms have been developed for coping with these challenges or, in systems analysis language, sources of system "disturbance."

The following chapters provide examples of the particular problems that are present in contemporary international politics and the specific means of preventing and limiting conflict in the international system. Chapter 3 is a discussion of the most serious international tensions that presently beset us; and Chapter 4 is an examination of the strengths and weaknesses of the specific mechanisms and procedures at the global level available for containing the disruptive forces of these tensions.

SUGGESTED READINGS

Aron, Raymond. *Peace and War*. Garden City, N.Y.: Doubleday, 1977.

Dougherty, James E., and Robert L. Pfaltzgraff, Jr. *Contending Theories of International Relations*. Philadelphia: Lippincott, 1971.

Keohane, Robert D., and Joseph S. Nye. *Power and Interdependence: World Politics in Transition*. Boston: Little, Brown, 1977.

Lieber, Robert J. *Theory and World Politics*. Cambridge, Mass.: Winthrop Publishers, 1972.

Scott, Andrew M. *The Functioning of the International Political System*. New York: Macmillan, 1967.

Chapter 3
International Tensions

Whether viewed from the perspective of one or more of the states as actors, or seen from above as an international system, today's world is clearly beset by a host of problems. The safety and interests of the states in the system are endangered by a number of challenges that tax the resources and talents available to national governments. And the stability, even the existence, of the international system as a whole is constantly threatened by disruptive forces of great magnitude and complexity. There are three principal dimensions of present global tensions: First is the struggle between the East, led by the Soviet Union, and the West, led by the United States. This has been overt since shortly after World War II, though its roots go much further back in time. Second is the poverty and chronic instability that plague most of what has become known as the Third World, the underdeveloped countries of Latin America, Africa, the Middle East, and Asia, many of which were former colonies that are experiencing enormous difficulties in achieving statehood, stability, and economic and political development. Third is the global ecological crisis, which poses an imminent challenge to modern society as we know it and may even threaten species survival. We will examine these three problems of our time, try to convey some idea of their gravity, and show how they are, in some important respects, linked.

The East–West Struggle

At the end of World War II the major states of Western Europe were virtually crippled, unable even to do anything about the dissolution of their overseas empires. Only the United States and, to a lesser extent, its wartime ally the Soviet Union emerged as powerful states facing each other uneasily across a devastated Europe. Before long, relations between these two newly superior world powers had degenerated into mutual suspicion, fear, and hostility. Some attempt to identify the origins and trace the course of this troubled relationship will aid in an understanding of its present status and likely future.

Origins

The peculiar wartime alliance that most people hoped would continue after Hitler had been defeated was probably always doomed to come unstuck eventually. Relations between major states are usually uneasy and tense. Even if the Soviet Union and the United States had had similar values, traditions, ideologies, and political systems; and even if relations between these two giants had been quite good during the 30 years following the Bolshevik seizure of power in 1917, these two states would probably have become suspicious, even hostile, rivals following World War II. In fact, their natural antagonism was heightened by sharply different and conflicting political and economic systems, traditions, values, and ideologies. Furthermore, at least since 1917, each side had quite often acted in such a way as to aggravate the antagonisms and strengthen the worst suspicions and fears held by the other side.

To the West, and perhaps especially to an often self-righteous United States inexperienced in world affairs, the Soviet Union was an evil and dangerous nation. The USSR, in this view, was a cold, closed, intensely secretive society whose 200 million people were ruled by a brutal, totalitarian regime. Russia's leaders, from Ivan the Terrible to Stalin, were seen as cynical, cruel, arrogant, unprincipled—even uncivilized—tyrants. Further, despite the incredible losses and reverses of the civil-war period from 1917 to 1920, the economic disasters during the 1920s and 1930s, Stalin's purges of the 1930s, and finally World War II, the Soviet Union had emerged, almost miraculously, as a powerful state with a strong industrial base, a competent though brutal central government, and a large modern army. The West feared that the communist rulers in Moscow would continue to seek such traditional Russian objectives as friendly if not subservient regimes in central Europe, the demilitarization of Russia's frequent foe Germany, warm-water ports, and a "fair share" in the European exploitation of East Asia.

In addition, the fact that under its new rulers Russia had adopted the ideology of communism meant that Russian foreign policy would be even more dangerously ambitious. Communism —the economic and political philosophy of Marx as interpreted by Lenin and amended by Stalin—was seen as a clearly anti-Western, anticapitalistic, antidemocratic system of beliefs. It had scientific pretensions in that it claimed to have discovered the immutable laws that governed historical progress and that enabled infallible predictions about the future. It was utopian in that it envisaged a glorious, perfect future, free of all the alleged defects and miseries of capitalist societies. It made its followers violently inclined, because it insisted this perfect society could only come about through violent clashes between the defenders of the old order and the vanguard revolutionaries.

It seemed at times to promise world war, because the Soviet Union was often pictured as the vanguard state that would eventually clash violently with the states of the old order to usher in the world of communism. And communism was an optimistic, confident, patient ideology, too; sooner or later, even if the Soviet Union did not help speed up the process, communism would prevail worldwide, as each capitalist state collapsed under the weight of uncorrectable internal structural weaknesses, or "contradictions." To the extent that this dynamic ideology determined Moscow's foreign policy, the West would be endangered and threatened. The West had enough to fear from a strong Soviet Union pursuing *traditional* Russian goals; if Moscow's rulers embarked on a crusade to spread its new faith and save the world, that policy would clearly be much more serious.

Thus, the Soviet Union appeared rather frightening to the West. And many of Moscow's actions reinforced the West's worst fears and suspicions. Before, during, and immediately following World War II, the Soviet Union did things that the West interpreted as provocative. Immediately upon taking power in 1917, the new Bolshevik regime called for similar uprisings in the other states of Europe. Then Lenin withdrew Russia from World War I, making a separate peace with the German empire, which was thereby enabled to concentrate all its energies and troops on the war against the Western allies. Following the war the Soviet Union defied commonly accepted practice when it refused to pay the czar's debts. In 1919 Lenin created the Communist International, or Comintern, a frankly subversive organization designed to hasten the coming of the communist millennium. In 1922 the West looked on apprehensively as the Rapallo Treaty was signed between the world's two outcast nations, Germany and the Soviet Union. During the 1920s and 1930s Stalin's brutal domestic policies in agriculture and industry, as well as his ruthless purges of real and fancied political opponents, disgusted and alarmed the West. Rapallo made the West apprehensive; the cynical 1939 Nazi–Soviet Nonaggression Treaty left Hitler free to conquer Western Europe and confirmed the apprehension. Then, late in 1939, in accordance with the deal Hitler and Stalin had made, the Soviet Union attacked Finland and seized the eastern half of Poland. Later, Hitler, in one of his more foolish moves, attacked the Soviet Union, which then quickly became an ally of Britain and the United States in the effort to stop the Nazi war machine.

Even during World War II, though, there were disturbing hints of the likely shape of future East–West relations: sharply differing views on the subject of postwar boundaries and political forms emerged and were never really resolved at the wartime conferences; and Stalin insisted, often in the most surly and insulting language, that his Western allies take some of the pressure off the Soviet Union by opening a second front against Hitler in 1942 or 1943, a year or two earlier than the Normandy invasion eventually took place. At the end of the war, the West could only helplessly and angrily watch as the Red Army enforced communization of most of Eastern and Central Europe, including the Soviet zone of conquered Germany.

Between 1946 and 1948 the Soviet Union assisted guerrilla operations in Greece, had to be pressured into withdrawing its occupation army from northern Iran, pressed aggressively but unsuccessfully for concessions from Turkey that would have turned Turkey into a Soviet puppet state, engineered a communist coup that ousted a democratic government in Czechoslovakia, and precipitated a major East–West confrontation by closing off the Western Powers' ground access to joint-occupied Berlin, 100 miles inside the Soviet zone of Germany. By 1947 or 1948, then, what came to be called the Cold War was clearly on; and Western observers laid most of the blame for the sorry state of affairs at Moscow's door.

On the other hand, the West appeared to the Soviet Union to be evil and dangerous. Moscow in 1917 saw the West as a collection of corrupt, decadent, unreliable, capitalist states. The Bolshevik leaders correctly assumed from the outset that these Western Capitalist states would be hostile to the first communist regime. The traditionally suspicious Russians, led first by the shrewd Lenin and later by the virtually paranoid Stalin, recognized that their country was not only weakened and vulnerable but also surrounded by stronger states. So, from Moscow's viewpoint, the West appeared to be just as objectionable and menacing as the Soviet Union appeared to the West.

· And, in instance after instance between 1917 and 1947, the West managed to reinforce Moscow's worst fears and suspicions. From 1917 to 1920, the new communist regime was desperately trying to consolidate its power by eliminating opposition forces in a civil war. During that time the West not only castigated the new regime for refusing to continue the war against Germany, but also intervened militarily on Soviet soil to try to bring down the new regime. United States and British troops assisted the White Russian forces in this struggle against the Red Army for two years before finally withdrawing. Next the new regime was kept out of the Versailles Peace Conference, as well as initially excluded from the new League of Nations. For years the leading Western states refused to have diplomatic or economic relations with the new regime, hoping that this *cordon sanitaire* would not only protect the West from what Clemenceau called the "germs of Bolshevism in the East," but also cripple the regime and cause it to collapse. Later, Moscow interpreted the West's appeasement of Hitler at Munich as a green light for Hitler to move East. At the same time the Western states seemed to be ignoring (or maybe even assisting) Japan's seizure of Manchuria and its attacks on Siberia. Then, although the members of the League of Nations had done next to nothing about Japanese, Italian, and German aggressions, the Soviet Union was sanctimoniously expelled from the League following its seizure of strategic portions of Finland, a seizure that could, unlike the fascists' attacks, be interpreted as at least somewhat defensive in nature, since Finland was flirting with Nazi Germany.

During World War II the British and Americans often gave Stalin the impression that they would like to see Nazi Germany and Bolshevik Russia destroy each other. Western delays in establishing the second front, secret British and United States attempts to negotiate peace with the Germans, and Western opposition at the wartime allied conferences to what Stalin saw as perfectly legitimate and deserved postwar Soviet territorial and political objectives all seemed to Stalin like the actions of potential antagonists rather than loyal allies.

Following the war, too, it seemed to Stalin that his erstwhile allies were determined to thwart the outcomes for which the Soviet Union had fought so long with such incredible sacrifices. The West not only vigorously opposed the sovietization of Eastern Europe but also demanded the creation of governments that, in Stalin's opinion, would inevitably have been hostile to the Soviet Union; the United States abruptly terminated its aid to Stalin; the Baruch Plan to control atomic weapons was viewed as a scheme to freeze United States monopoly in this obviously vital field; and the new United Nations was quickly shaping up as an anticommunist organization dominated by the United States—an organization where the Soviet Union would quite often be left no alternative but to use its Security Council veto. Before long the United States was actively opposing the guerrilla communist operations in Greece; leaping to Turkey's defense; promising to assist other states troubled by revolution or subversion; rearming themselves and, worse yet, Germany; and forming military pacts and alliances with a number of the states surrounding the USSR. From the Soviet perspective, these actions—before, during, and after World War II—all served to confirm Moscow's belief in the inevitable hostility of the West.

It is really impossible to say which side's fears were most provocative. Assigning an exact percentage of the blame for the cold war to each side would likewise be impossible. Truth in these matters is, like beauty, in the eye of the beholder. And admitting that the fears felt by both sides were to some extent justified does not imply approval of either side's system or ideology or actions. It is possible and necessary, on the other hand, to recognize that these *mutual* fears and suspicions existed and to some extent determined Soviet and Western policies. It is, after all, not reality that shapes policy, but rather government leaders' perceptions of reality; and these perceptions are unavoidably based on incomplete and imperfect information that is distorted by the leaders' biases and advisers. At any rate, by 1948, the cold war had emerged as a full-blown East–West schism.

While the basically uneasy character of East–West relations has remained the same in the past thirty-odd years, the relationship has moved through several phases. In general, there seems to have been a gradual decline in the level of tensions over the years, though the reduction has been slow and uneven.

Phase 1: Belligerence

The first phase, lasting roughly ten years from the end of World War II to about 1956, was a period of high tension and intense mutual fears and suspicions. Soviet moves in Eastern Europe, Iran, and Turkey; Soviet assistance to the communist partisans in the Greek civil war; the Soviet-triggered Berlin crisis of 1948; the 1948 communist coup in Czechoslovakia; the fall of China into communist hands in 1949; and the North Korean invasion of South Korea in June, 1950, all served to convince the West that there was a communist monolith head-quartered in Moscow, bent on conquering the world, or at least a prostrate and exhausted Western Europe.

The West, primarily the United States, energetically responded to these developments. President Truman enunciated what became known as the Truman Doctrine, promising "to support free peoples who are resisting attempted subjugation by armed minorities or by outside pressures." United States economic aid was poured into Greece and Turkey and, through the Marshall Plan, into Western Europe to rebuild the war-torn states as bulwarks against communism. Later, the United States took the lead in creating a collection of military alliances designed to "contain" Soviet expansionist tendencies: the North Atlantic Treaty Organization (NATO), the Southeast Asia Treaty Organization (SEATO), and the Central Treaty Organization (CENTO). Bilateral defensive pacts between the United States and numerous other noncommunist states were also signed during the 1950s. The United States undertook almost the entire burden of responding to the North Korean invasion with, eventually, the goal of ousting the communist North Korean government and forcefully reunifying that small country that had emerged divided from World War II. This ambitious undertaking was eventually thwarted by China's entry into the Korean War. Since the armistice arranged in 1953, the Korean peninsula has remained divided along the 38th parallel, a constant symbol—like divided Germany in the

West—of the East–West cleavage and a constant danger point in world politics. Meanwhile, the United Nations had been converted by the Korean War and other anticommunist activities into an organization dominated by the United States and often inimical to Soviet interests and goals.

Accompanying these United States military and economic responses was a rhetorical crusade to match communist ideological bombast. President Eisenhower's secretary of state, John Foster Dulles, promised loosely to "liberate" the "captive peoples" of Eastern Europe and to "roll back" the iron curtain, talked of "unleashing" and assisting the Chinese Nationalists on Taiwan to reconquer mainland China, sought to enlist the people of the "free world" in a crusade to crush "atheistic" communism, and accused the leaders of the underdeveloped world who sought to remain aloof from the East–West fray of being "immoral." And in the United States, Senator Joseph McCarthy exploited popular fears and frustrations to conduct a witch hunt for communists in high office—a witch hunt that pushed policy and policy makers into a sterile and rigidly doctrinaire anticommunism.

Phase 2: Coexistence

By the mid-1950s the religious zeal of both sides showed signs of diminishing. The second phase of East–West relations, from about 1956 to 1963, can be fairly characterized as an era of emergent, if uneasy, coexistence. Each side demonstrated the beginnings of tolerance.

By its inaction when the Soviet Union crushed uprisings in East Germany (1953) and Hungary (1956), the United States demonstrated that it would not interfere in Soviet-bloc affairs or risk a clash with Moscow on behalf of Dulles's hollow rhetorical promises. Next, Moscow and Washington even cooperated actively in the effort to defuse the dangerous Suez crisis of late 1956 brought on by the British–French–Israeli attack on Egypt. Stalin's successors—he had died in March, 1953—seemed to be less ambitious, more sober . . . almost, some said, more businesslike.

In addition, by the late 1950s Western Europe and Japan

had been rebuilt and those governments did not feel quite so vulnerable to Soviet seizure. Also, by the late 1950s serious fissures had appeared in the communist bloc: Yugoslavia had broken away earlier, Hungary had shown its independent spirit briefly, and China was no longer a dependable instrument of Moscow policy. Western observers looking eastward no longer saw the unity of enemies as quite so monolithic. True, Moscow did develop thermonuclear weapons by the early 1950s and intercontinental missiles by the end of the decade. But even this new fact may have induced some moderation into the East–West struggle: the Soviet leaders quickly sensed what subsequently became known as the balance of terror, and sensed its meaning—that major war between the two superpowers would amount to mutual suicide. This realization that war with the United States and its allies had been eliminated as a rational policy option was quite sobering, perhaps even stabilizing. And finally, during this period, the decline of Stalinism in the Soviet Union was matched by a corresponding decline of McCarthyism in the United States. Both great states were then to some extent freed of ideological impediments to rational policy making.

Phase 2 was not, of course, entirely without its episodes of crisis and potential armed conflict between the superpowers: a Berlin crisis in 1961 that included the dramatic erection of the infamous Berlin wall; the civil conflicts in Laos, the Congo, and Lebanon with the superpowers taking opposing sides; Castro's successful seizure of power in Cuba in the western hemisphere; and the beginnings of the United States involvement in Vietnam. But, even when times were tense, the superpowers both displayed less emotionalism and ideological fervor than they had shown several years earlier; each revealed a corresponding increase in tolerance, caution, and interest in diplomatic, rather than military or rhetorical, approaches to managing their disagreements.

Phase 3: Détente

The third phase of the troubled U.S.–USSR relationship, which began around 1963 and lasted until the late 1970s, has been aptly characterized as one of emerging détente between the two superpowers. Each maintained its defensive posture, based on continued suspicions and backed by awesome military might (see Table 3.1 and Table 3.2). But each also seemed more willing to move beyond the rather negative stance of coexistence and the still aloof attitude of simple tolerance. Each seemed increasingly interested in developing the cooperative element in a relationship that continued to contain a competi-

Table 3.1 At a Glance: Military Resources of NATO, Warsaw Pact, and the People's Republic of China

	NATO	Warsaw Pact	People's Republic of China
Population	554,800,000	365,700,000	900,000,000
GNP	$3,367 billion	$1,240 billion	$309 billion
Military Spending	$175 billion	$139 billion	$23–28 billion
Military Manpower	4,900,000	4,850,000*	4,300,000
Strategic Nuclear Weapons	9,400	4,500	200?
Tactical Nuclear Weapons	22,000?	15,000?	N.A.
Tanks	25,250+	59,000	9,000
Antitank Missiles	200,000+	N.A.	N.A.
Other Armor Vehicles	48,000+	62,000+	3,500
Heavy Artillery	11,400+	22,600+	20,000
Combat Aircraft	8,900+	10,400	5,900
Helicopters	12,300	4,550	350
Major Surface Warships	522	247	22
Attack Submarines (all types)	211	239	66

* The U.S. Defense Department estimates of Warsaw Pact manpower includes 750,000 uniformed civilian personnel making the total Warsaw Pact manpower 5.6 million.
Source: Center for Defense Information, "NATO and the Neutron Bomb," *The Defense Monitor,* June, 1978, p. 6.

tive element as well. Both these superpowers seemed more interested than they had been earlier in seeking areas of common interest where mutually advantageous accommodations might be arranged.

Paradoxically, this improved climate came only on the heels of one of the most serious East–West confrontations, the Cuban missile crisis of the autumn of 1962. And in a way this most grave episode may have been useful, perhaps even indispensable, for ushering in a period of détente. Khrushchev, in an amazing gamble that may have convinced his colleagues that he was too rash and thus may have cost him his job, decided to place nuclear missiles in communist Cuba; success in this venture would have redressed an unfavorable weaponry balance and humiliated the United States and its new, young president, John F. Kennedy, in one dramatic gesture. But Kennedy met the challenge with military counterthreats, forced the withdrawal of the Soviet missiles, and dealt a severe blow to the prestige of both Khrushchev and the Soviet Union. Perhaps most importantly, however, the crisis seemed to convince Moscow that Washington expected the same respect for the Western sphere of influence that the West had shown for the Soviet sphere during the 1956 Hungarian uprising. On that occasion the West had fussed and fumed but had nonetheless studiously avoided a major clash over what was clearly regarded, though certainly not labeled, an internal family quarrel in the Soviet sphere.

Table 3.2   Four Major Military Indicators

	Anti-Soviet (U.S., other NATO, China)	Soviet (Warsaw Pact)
Strategic Nuclear Weapons	10,500	6,000
Military Spending (1979)	$265 billion	$175 billion
Military Personnel	9.5 million	4.8 million
Major Surface Ships	445	235

Source: Center for Defense Information, "American Strength, Soviet Weakness," *The Defense Monitor*, June, 1980, p. 4.

Once Moscow was willing to similarly recognize the West's sphere and refrain from attacking or entering it, the superpowers could settle down in a live-and-let-live way to bargain over problems of joint interest. The 1962 Cuban missile crisis may have clarified the limits and rules of the relationship for the Soviet Union just as Hungary had for the United States; it thus fulfilled a useful purpose and may have made détente possible if not inevitable, since there were a number of important areas where Soviet and United States interests coincided, making agreements or at least tacit understandings possible.

The most important of these areas was that of arms control. (See Figure 3.1.) Each superpower recognized its ability to do lethal damage to the other, even in retaliation after "riding out" an initial surprise attack; both were aware that thermonuclear

Figure 3.1 Total Strategic Weapons of the United States and the USSR, 1960–1978.

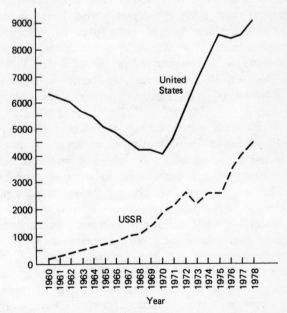

Source: (Center for Defense Information. *The Defense Monitor:* July, 1978, p. 1.)

war would be mutually suicidal. Each understood its clear interest in averting this catastrophe by stabilizing the arms balance, by leveling off or even reducing its respective strategic arsenal. Each also seemed interested in saving some of the enormous sums of money it was spending on armaments that might be invested in other sectors of its economy. These shared views led in 1969 to the initiation of the strategic arms limitation talks (SALT), which resulted during the 1970s in a number of complex formal USSR–U.S. agreements limiting and controlling these weapons of mass destruction. The Americans and Russians agreed to both quantitative and qualitative limits on their respective arsenals in these bilateral negotiations that might yield even further results. Moreover, both countries seemed sensitive to the danger of deploying particular weapons which could only be used in a surprise attack and which, therefore, the other side could only regard as provocative and destabilizing; this recognition led to instances of unilateral restraint. Each country also went ahead unilaterally to build in safeguards against war caused by miscalculation, accident, or unauthorized actions by subordinates. And the two major nuclear states collaborated on the Test Ban Treaty, the Nuclear Non-Proliferation Treaty, and other schemes to dissuade potential nuclear states from acquiring these dangerous weapons.

East–West trade was a second area of coinciding interests. Although the Soviet Union had made impressive strides in the rapid industrialization of its economy, it was still not self-sufficient in agriculture, particularly in years of poor harvests when it had to purchase food abroad; the much more productive American farmer was happy to meet this demand. And the Soviet leadership was eager to purchase some kinds of sophisticated technologies from the United States, such as oil-drilling equipment, computers, and manufacturing plants. Other deals involving sales of finished manufactured goods and consumer items were also made. Each side benefited from these trade deals, though the terms of trade overwhelmingly favored the United States; and, as trading increased, it was hoped that tensions might correspondingly decline.

Paralleling these commercial arrangements was a great increase during the 1970s in technical, scientific, and cultural cooperation, involving joint explorations of space; joint research projects in oceanography, ecology, and medicine; exchange visits of farmers, businesspeople, and artists; and freer exchanges of information, documents, and studies in a range of disciplines. Again, it was hoped that these cooperative activities would promote a reduction in tensions between the superpowers.

Despite these elements of cooperation or détente during the 1970s, important differences remained and continue into the 1980s. The Soviet Union has not, and will not, become an open society with a Western-style democratic political system. More importantly, the Soviet Union has not abandoned its fundamental foreign-policy objectives, a combination of common state goals, historic Russian desires, and newer communist dreams; pursuing these ends will bring the Soviet Union into frequent clashes with its neighbors and Western states with their different, sometimes incompatible, objectives. The rulers in the Kremlin will continue to resent, too, American efforts, escalated in the late 1970s, to pressure them for changes in the sensitive areas of human rights and internal domestic politics. Finally, the Soviet Union's apparent determination to achieve full global superpower status and to develop its influence around the world has alarmed many in the West who had grown accustomed to unchallenged superiority on the global stage. A significant Soviet arms build-up since the mid-1960s has prompted United States efforts to retain its strategic superiority (or, as some would have it, to regain its lost edge), fueling yet another round in the arms race and jeopardizing East–West trade and arms control efforts. Soviet involvement in the continuing Middle East drama and in some civil and border wars in Africa were further irritants, especially to some who had always thought that détente was a mistake, a one-way street that favored Soviet diplomacy. Particularly distressing to the West was Moscow's invasion of Afghanistan in late 1979 to prop up a tottering puppet regime in that strategically located Islamic country on the Soviet Union's southern border, close to the Persian Gulf oil so important to the Western industrialized economies. In response, the United States terminated some commercial ties, shelved the strategic arms limitation treaty that had been languishing in the United States Senate, and led a boycott of the 1980 Olympic games held in Moscow.

Prospects

The East–West struggle is not over; the two camps continue to fear, distrust, and antagonize each other. But we have come some distance from the days when each side felt it unnecessary, impossible, and even immoral to deal calmly with the other. East–West relations continue to follow a bumpy course, though the general, long-term trends seem encouraging, if for no other reason than that everyone recognizes that the alternative to coexistence is catastrophe, that we must all live together in peace on this smallish planet or we shall all perish together.

Even if this hopeful analysis is basically accurate and not based on wishful thinking, the East–West struggle is still a most dangerous phenomenon of world politics that needs constant attention and prudent management. For while the tensions may have diminished since the 1950s, while sobriety may have overtaken ideological passion on both sides, and while the *likelihood* of armed clash between the superpowers may have lessened, the *consequences* of such an armed clash would be vastly more serious now than they would have been 10 to 20 years ago. If the Soviet Union and the Western nations found themselves in a shooting war now, it is quite probable that nuclear weapons would be used early on. Once this nuclear threshold is crossed, several thousand bombers and intercontinental missiles bearing thermonuclear weapons would probably soon follow, laying waste to most of the United States, as well as Eastern and Western Europe. Several hundred million people would die quickly. Another several hundred million would die shortly thereafter from radiation poisoning and the chaotic anarchy that a major nuclear exchange would leave in its wake everywhere. Civilization would suffer a blow from which it probably would not recover. And the long-term effects that such a cataclysmic episode would have on social organizations and even planetary life itself are simply incalculable. Moreover, even thermonuclear weapons may not be the ultimate in the ongoing search for ingenious weaponry. "Progress" is being contemplated in weather control and biological warfare that may yet render thermonuclear weapons obsolete; artificially created floods, earthquakes, hurricanes, and plagues may one day soon be available to the feuding superpowers. Thus, it is fortunate that East–West relations have improved somewhat, but not particularly comforting. The world's scientists have perhaps more than offset any increase in moderation shown by the world's statesmen.

The Third World

Ranking alongside the continuing East–West struggle as a major source of global tensions is the instability prevailing in the Third World, that is, in the underdeveloped countries of Latin America, Africa, the Middle East, and Asia. We shall attempt to deal with three dimensions of the agonies of the Third World: two of the more important regional disputes, the chronic underdevelopment and poverty of most Third World countries, and the growing struggle between the wealthy countries of the northern hemisphere and the poor countries of the southern hemisphere.

Regional Disputes

Though the principal threat to global stability (and even human survival) remains the threat of nuclear war between the superpowers, several other significant international disputes of long standing continue to fester, perhaps most importantly among them the Arab–Israeli confrontation and the racial conflicts in southern Africa. This short book cannot delve deeply into these intricate and tragic imbroglios; but a brief note on each will at least demonstrate its potential for threatening regional, and even world, stability and peace.

In 1948 the new state of Israel was created out of a section of Palestine which had been a British mandate since World War I. Israel has been at war since 1948 with various of its neighbors, the Arab states that surround it and which argue that Israel has wrongfully seized Arab lands. Large-scale armed hostilities have erupted four times—in 1948, 1956, 1967, and 1973—only to end inconclusively each time, as the Arabs suffered military reverses and as Israel regrouped to prepare for the anticipated next encounter. Between wars, both sides engage in raids, sabotage, terrorism, assassination, reprisals, other lower-scale military activities, and threatening gestures . . . as well as in on-again, off-again diplomatic talks aimed at accomplishing their respective, and mostly incompatible, objectives.

Israel seeks firm assurances that its Arab neighbors have finally accepted Israel's continued existence in their midst and wants these assurances backed up by complete normalization of relations among all these countries and by agreed-upon arrangements for militarily secure borders. Israel wants to retain some of the territories seized from Egypt, Syria, and Jordan during the 1967 war, arguing that retention is necessary for security or political or religious reasons. Israel suggests that the problem of the Palestinian refugees could be solved by the Palestinians either moving to one or another of the twenty-odd Arab countries or agreeing to live as citizens of Israel, accepting the Jewish nature of the state.

For their part, the Arabs are determined to retrieve all (or nearly all) of the territories they lost in 1967. Some of the more militant Arab leaders appear not to have come yet to accept an Israel in their midst; even the most conciliatory have difficulty envisaging harmonious, normalized relations for years to come. Arabs want the Palestinian problem solved by the establishment of yet another state in the crowded region, a sovereign Palestinian state perhaps occupying land on the west bank of the Jordan River now held by Israel; but the Israelis are not willing to see a threatening Palestinian state created there.

No end is in sight. Very wide differences continue between the disputants, which occasional flurries of diplomatic activity tend sometimes to obscure. Each side is armed with increasingly destructive weaponry purchased in the international arms bazaar or contributed by outside countries with emotional or economic or political interests to advance. Passions remain high; the confrontation has become something of a holy war, for which a durable compromise settlement that each party could accept sometimes seems farther off than ever.

A second cauldron of tensions that promises to continue getting a share of the headlines throughout the 1980s is southern Africa, where the legacy of colonialism is white minority governments clinging to power over increasingly militant black majority populations in several countries. Though the 1974 military coup in Portugal quickly resulted in independence for the Portuguese colonies of Mozambique and Angola, the most difficult and most explosive situations remain.

South Africa's 4 million whites exercise virtually absolute economic and political control in that country, even though they are outnumbered five to one by 18 million blacks, 2 million "coloreds" (persons of mixed race), and about 700,000 Asians. Most of the whites are Afrikaners of Dutch, French, and German descent, who settled in the sparsely populated southern tip of Africa in the 1650s, just after black tribes had begun to move south into the region. For over a century South Africa was a British colony, becoming in 1934 a self-governing British dominion like Canada, and then withdrawing from the Commonwealth in 1971 as the other Commonwealth members became more and more critical of South Africa's racial policies. South Africa's government has been controlled since 1948 by the Nationalist Party, dominated by the Afrikaners and staunchly committed to the policy of *apartheid,* or separate development of the races, with whites to remain in complete control of South Africa's political and economic life while blacks would exercise limited rule in black homelands, or Bantustans, scattered bits of land composing the roughly 13 percent of South Africa's territory which the South African government has set aside for the black 70 percent of the population. At the national level, blacks have—and, if the government prevails, would continue to have—minimal political or civil rights, severely limited educational or occupational opportunities, and correspondingly low living standards. They are subjected to a brutal oppression by the powerful security bureaucracy of the white regime, which relies on the usual police-state methods of preventive detention, sham judicial proceedings, torture, censorship, required identity cards, and so forth. Predictably, this situation has provoked not only the condemnation of most of the world's other states but also a black nationalist movement determined to bring majority rule to South Africa. However, the South African regime is powerfully armed to resist and suppress the black insurgency, which is not well organized. And outside pressures on the regime have so far been mostly ineffective. South Africa is strong enough to successfully resist most pressures; and the countries most capable of asserting some leverage on South Africa—Britain and the United States—have been reluctant to press very hard, partly because of their very extensive investments in South Africa (6 billion dollars from Britain, 2 billion dollars from the United States) and partly because they have been seeking South Africa's help in solving the region's two other explosive problems: the disposition of Southwest Africa and the situation in Rhodesia.

Southwest Africa was a German colony until World War I, when it became a League of Nations mandate administered by South Africa. After World War II, South Africa's request for permission from the United Nations to legally annex the territory was refused by the world body; but, in defiance of the international community, South Africa has successfully retained control of the mineral-rich land with valuable Atlantic seaports. Again, the country's actions have provoked opposition not only from other countries, but also from black nationalists seeking independence for their country, which they call Namibia, and some form of majority rule politically. Finally, in mid-1978 both South Africa's government and the principal nationalist leaders accepted a Western plan for independence and majority rule for Namibia, though problems remain: important territorial issues are yet to be resolved, and the intense rivalries of contending nationalist leaders jeopardize a peaceful transition.

In neighboring Rhodesia, meanwhile, the white supremacist

regime of Ian Smith until 1980 governed the poor, landlocked, agrarian country whose population of about 6 million is only 4 percent white and 96 percent black. Following conquest late in the nineteenth century by British troops, Rhodesia was British-ruled until 1965, when the white colonial administration in Salisbury declared its independence from Britain. From 1965 until 1980 the Smith regime fought a steadily losing battle to maintain white rule. Condemned by the United Nations in 1965, living after that under severe economic sanctions agreed upon by the United Nations members, unrecognized by any other state, pressured to yield by its lifeline and main ally South Africa, under continuous prodding by Western governments, and besieged by escalating guerrilla warfare in the 1970s, the regime finally agreed in 1979 to yield power in elections, finally held in 1980, in which the country's blacks voted for the first time.

The overwhelming victor in these reasonably fair elections was Robert Mugabe, one of the black nationalist leaders who had directed the guerrilla war against Smith's regime during the 1970s from bases in the neighboring black-ruled states of Zambia and Mozambique. Mugabe formed a government and began the process of transferring government authority to blacks, uniting the black nationalist factions and tribes, healing the country's wounds, and trying to reassure Zimbabwe's nervous whites so they would not leave the country, taking their needed skills and assets with them. Though these are all formidable tasks and though black factionalism might yet replace white intransigence as the paramount threat to a peaceful Zimbabwe, it was at least possible in late 1981 to hope that this corner of unhappy southern Africa might be stabilizing.

There are other simmering disputes that might flare into the open to threaten global peace: relations between the Arab states are uneasy in the best of times; India and Pakistan, if no longer warring over Kashmir or religious questions, are not yet friends; Korea and Germany are still divided as a result of World War II, which ended nearly four decades ago; the situation in Southeast Asia continues to be marked by repression, uprooted peoples, famine, and warfare among the countries of the area, even following the departure of the French in the 1950s and the Americans in the 1970s; and, though not strictly a Third World dispute, the *other* cold war, between China and the Soviet Union over disputed territories along their 4500-mile-long border, as well as over various ideological questions, could erupt into armed hostilities threatening regional, even global, peace.

Moreover, sadly enough, like the two regional situations already sketched in somewhat greater detail, these other prospective clashes could all quite easily become holy wars, with resolvable or manageable policy differences transformed into clashes over basic principles and with the Righteous going forth to exorcise Evil.

Poverty and Underdevelopment

If anything, though, is more ominous than these present and future regional conflicts, it is the *internal* problems disrupting nearly every state in the Third World. Most of this domestic instability can be traced to the grinding poverty to be found in most Third World countries. This explosive poverty, in turn, has many roots; to some extent it is the result of local factors, to some extent it is the result of worldwide technological changes, and to some extent it is a legacy of colonial rule and the relationships between the conquerors and the conquered that were established in the colonial period and have influenced today's relationships between newly independent countries and the former colonial powers.

In most Third World countries most of the people live in abject poverty, lacking the basic necessities of human survival: food, shelter from the elements, medical care (see Figure 3.2). Hence, infant mortality is high; it is common in many Third World countries for every fifth baby born to die of malnutrition or disease before it reaches its first birthday. Adults starving to death is also a worldwide commonplace, with an estimated 10 to 20 million people dying in this cruel way each year. Malnutrition is even more widespread; the Food and Agriculture Organization estimates that between one-third and one-half of

Figure 3.2 The Gap Between Developed and Less Developed Countries.

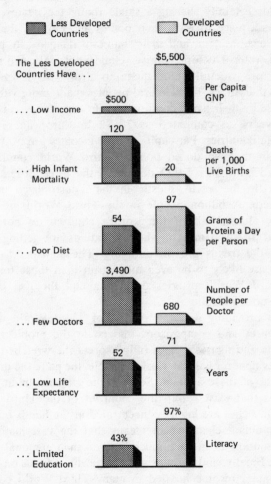

The Development Gap

Source: (U.S. Agency for International Development, *AID's Challenge in an Interdependent World*. Washington, D.C.: Agency for International Development, 1977, p. 19.)

the world's 4 billion people suffer from inadequate diets so that their physical and mental development is stunted, their energies sapped, their educability impaired, their hope destroyed. Most of these unfortunate creatures live in huts and hovels, often with a large family sharing a single room; the nearest stream triples as a place to wash their bodies and clothes, their community sewer system, and their source of dangerously polluted drinking water. Doctors, dentists, clinics, hospitals, and medical supplies are woefully inadequate to deal with a variety of diseases that attack Third World peoples made more vulnerable to disease by their living conditions. Life expectancy is typically 45–50 years, as compared to 70–72 in European or North American countries. Per capita annual incomes are 500 dollars or less in the two dozen poorest Third World countries, as compared with over 5,000 dollars in the three dozen richest countries in the world, mostly in the industrialized northern hemisphere. A billion people in the Third World are totally illiterate, almost half of the world's children do not attend school at all. And most of these situations are getting worse, most of the trends are discouraging. The statistics for 1990 or 2000 are likely to be even more grim than those for 1980, with Third World miseries deepening and the gap between rich and poor widening.

While providing a useful picture of Third World agonies, these figures and comparisons understate the problem. First, cold facts and figures cannot fully express the wretched conditions prevalent for half the world's people, the pain, the intensity, the extent of these agonies. Second, the statistics hide the inequalities that exist *within* the countries of the Third World, where the riches are highly concentrated in the hands of a very small dominant class, which means that the vast majority of the population is in fact much poorer than national figures indicate. Finally, and perhaps most tragically, a focus on growth of per capita income has led in many Third World countries to policies, designed to stimulate growth, which have often had adverse consequences for the living conditions of ordinary citizens.

Compounding the problem of Third World poverty is the

dramatic increase in the world's population, especially in under-developed countries (see Figure 3.3). In the Stone Age the world's population was probably roughly 10 million. By the time of Christ it had reached 300 million. It took the next 1700 years to double to 600 million. But by 1960 the world's

Figure 3.3 Population Forecasts by Region, to the Year 2000.

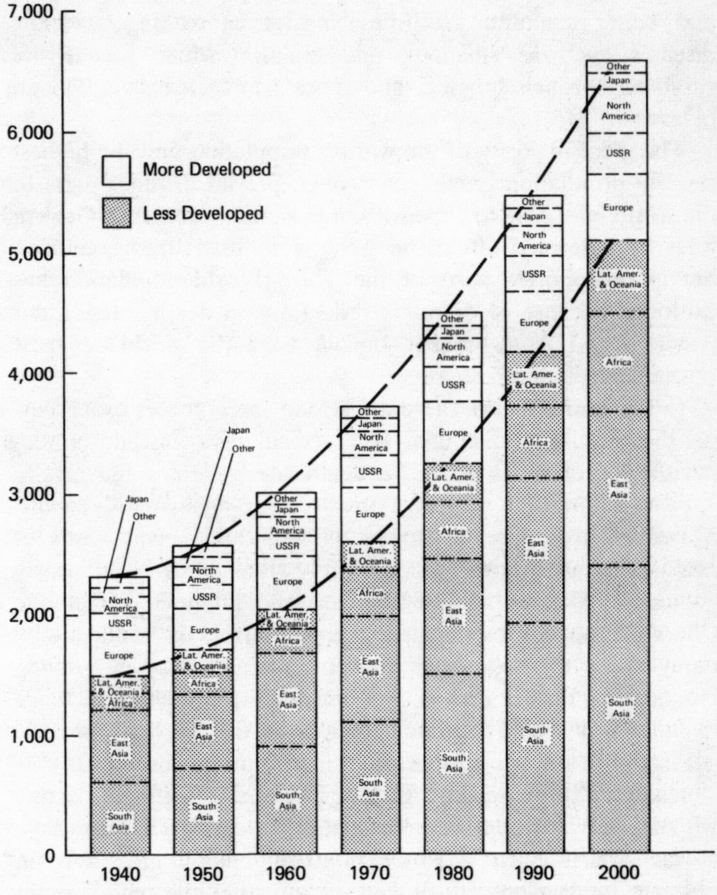

Source: (World Bank Group, *Trends in Developing Countries.* Washington, D.C.: International Bank for Reconstruction and Development, 1971.)

population was 3 billion and was growing at such an accelerated rate that it will take only 40 years to double (to more than 6 billion by the year 2000).

The reasons for the sharp acceleration in the world's population are many, but the most important contributing factor has been the sharp decline in death rates over the last 300 years as a consequence of the introduction of Western public-health measures aimed at providing pure water supplies and better sanitation facilities and at controlling epidemic diseases such as smallpox and malaria. More people are surviving through infancy, and more people are living to an older age.

The great majority of the world's population and the highest rates of population growth, moreover, prevail in those parts of the world least able to cope with the resultant problems. Growth rates have leveled off in the wealthy industrialized countries, but in the poorest parts of the Third World population has exploded because of dramatic reductions in death rates. Latin America and Asia (except Japan) have the world's highest rates of population increase.

In the Third World, there are strong social forces exacerbating the population dilemma. The medical advances and public-health programs that reduce the death rate are almost universally approved and given top priority for financial support. Moreover, there are enormous religious and social obstacles against any attempt to reduce sharply rising birth rates: nearly universal strictures against abortion and infanticide; Catholic Church disapproval of artificial birth control; the tendency by many males to use repeated fatherhood as a way of proving manhood; and, perhaps most importantly, widespread preference in the Third World for large families to till the land, provide parents with old-age support, and insure proper burial rites.

Historically, population growth rates have begun to decline with the development of industrialized society. Thus we have a classic vicious circle where rapid population growth is an obstacle to development and development is the most certain way to achieve a leveling off of population growth.

The population explosion has raised, directly or indirectly, serious problems for almost every government in the Third World. Inadequate food supply is probably the first among these. The prevailing primitive agricultural methods that dominate the local food production sector are simply not able to produce enough food for the people in these states; malnutrition and the resultant mental and physical deterioration, as well as death by starvation, are already widespread. Modern techniques of cultivation are to be found only in plantation agriculture for export, which also occupies the most fertile land and is often under foreign control, a direct heritage of the colonial past. If these richer lands were available to the local farmers in underdeveloped countries and if modernized production techniques were employed, they would begin to get results closer to those achieved in the Netherlands and Japan, and food production would rise appreciably. In addition to being relegated to the poorest land, another principal barrier to such efficient agriculture is the archaic system of land tenure prevalent in the Third World. Most of the world's peasants do not own their land, but are hopelessly in debt to money lenders and absentee landlords who are too often disinclined to invest even a small part of their profits to improve productivity. Furthermore, over the centuries the land has been divided up into tiny parcels that cannot support the equipment used in mechanized farming. Land reform is clearly a first requisite for increasing agricultural productivity and even for general economic development in these still predominantly agricultural economies; but enormously powerful vested interests stand in the way of such needed change. Also, serious technical difficulties combine with cultural resistance to make dramatic production improvements unlikely in the near future, although new irrigation techniques and the discovery of "miracle" high-yield grains are promising. But even if production were to become miraculously adequate, the storage, processing, and distribution facilities would not be able to get the food from the fields and into the bellies of the starving masses. India and Cambodia have both had difficulties in unloading, storing, and distributing the relief grain shipments they have received. Food shortage is perhaps the most serious and destabilizing aspect of underdevelopment; starving citizens are inevitably threats to domestic order.

A second set of problems that the population explosion has either raised or accentuated for the regimes of the Third World is nearly as serious: urban crowding and the attendant increased demand for governmental services. Calcutta, India, for example, probably has more than 17 million inhabitants, though no accurate census is possible. It has recently been estimated that by the year 2000 most of the world's largest cities will be in the underdeveloped world; Mexico City is predicted to be the world's largest city, with an expected population of 35 million. Many, if not most, of these urban dwellers are former farmers and villagers who left the overpopulated countryside because it could not support them, only to find themselves unemployed burdens on the urban political authorities suddenly responsible for trying to provide schools, welfare, housing, transportation systems, health care, pure water, food, and even jobs for this exploding and restless constituency. The urban problems presently being experienced in North America and Western Europe pale in comparison to those of many Third World nations. The whole world is undergoing an unsettling shift from rural to urban life; in Third World states—where most cities are not even established, organized, industrial centers with some jobs and at least rudimentary public services—this transition is extremely turbulent.

Much of the poverty plaguing the Third World is attributable to local conditions, to serious deficiencies common to most of these new societies. There is a real shortage and sometimes a complete absence of the fundamental social, political, and economic ingredients so necessary for stability: national unity, an effective central government, and basic economic structures and factors.

Many of the new governments are fragile and weak chiefly because the states themselves do not correspond with historical and social realities. They are lacking a sense of national community and loyalty to transcend narrower communities and allegiances. Nationalism, once thought to be such a potent force in the Third World, turns out to have been potent mainly in a negative sense as a force that was able to unite disparate factions for the task of ousting the European colonialists; once that great unifying struggle was won, however, nationalism's positive, constructive power was found to be quite low, as old factionalisms emerged to thwart consolidation of the victory over the Europeans.

Virtually every state in the Third World includes large unassimilable minorities that are constant sources of irritation and occasionally of fragmentation and civil war. The minorities may be tribal groups, like the Ibos of Nigeria who felt persecuted enough to declare their region's independence, thus precipitating the civil war between Nigeria and secessionist Biafra that raged for nearly three years from May, 1967, to January, 1970. Or the minorities may be religious groups such as the remaining Moslems in India. They may be ethnic or national in character, like the Indians and the blacks in Latin America, the Turks in Cyprus, and the overseas Chinese spread throughout Southeast Asia. They may be linguistic units, such as the dozens of non-Hindi language groups in India that necessitate India's parliament to conduct most of its business in English, the only common language.

This social heterogeneity is due largely to the artificial and arbitrary boundaries drawn when the European colonial powers were dividing up the spoils 200 years ago with no regard for local religious, ethnic, or linguistic realities. Usually the leaders of the independence movements after World War II had little alternative but to accept these artificial colonial boundaries as the borders of their new states; and many hoped to weld these new states into even larger political entities. But these movements—Pan Africanism, for example—have foundered as it becomes painfully clear that even the national bases for sovereign states often do not exist.

To make matters worse, the left-over colonial boundaries frequently divide a coherent minority unit or group between two or more states, thereby making it a source of international tensions, border clashes, and even war. Relations between the East African states of Ethiopia, Uganda, the Sudan, and

Somalia are strained because present boundaries cut through several different tribal areas. Also, many states are solicitous of the status and well-being of their ethnic compatriots in other countries, as for example, Turkey's concern for the Turkish Cypriot minority on the predominantly Greek Cypriot island of Cyprus just off Turkey's shores. Neighboring states, then, frequently have an emotional interest in meddling in each other's internal affairs to effect reunification of a divided group or to aid beleaguered compatriots.

These centrifugal tendencies would be enough in themselves to produce the chronically weak national governments that are so common in the Third World. But additional factors tend to aggravate their plight and thus contribute to persistent instability. Many of the new states not only adopted artificial colonial boundaries but also attempted to transplant essentially Western governmental forms to countries without the necessary societal foundations or experience to make these work. The departing Europeans, with the grudging or eager agreement of the European-educated nationalist leaders, imposed Western-style presidents, prime ministers, courts, bureaucracies, federal structures, political parties, school systems, and election procedures on populations that naturally regarded these new political arrangements as alien.

The new governments proceeded to vindicate this popular skepticism and hostility as they proved unable to meet the accelerated demands of growing urban populations, who were decreasingly stoic, decreasingly fatalistic, and increasingly militant. To some extent the failures are due to the sentimental Western creation of democratic governments when authoritarian central governments were probably necessary to ensure order and accomplish development. And to some extent the failures were also due to widespread corruption from top to bottom in numerous national administrations. Furthermore, the masses of the Third World have traditionally been indifferent and hostile toward government—which has usually been correctly identified with the tax collector and the oppressor, and has been or has seemed to have been the tool of the landlords and moneylenders. And tactics successful in the anticolonial struggles for liberation taught the lesson to all—masses and elites alike—that obstructionism and even violence were effective tools to use to achieve political ends.

All of this body of experience adds up to numerous governments that lack respect, allegiance, obedience, and support from their populations. Numerous Third World governments are generally regarded, by citizens who are increasingly willing to take to the streets for remedies, as alien, illegitimate, impotent, incompetent, and corrupt. And these attitudes toward any government in office are usually shared by some military officers and opposition politicians likewise willing to employ violence to attain power through a coup d'etat or even a thoroughgoing revolution. Almost daily the newspapers report such collapses and changes of weak governments in fragile new states, alongside similar reports of civil strife afflicting others.

In addition to national cohesion and an effective central government, a society—to maintain stability and overcome underdevelopment—must have an adequate economic system. Most of the Third World countries lack one or more of the essential components of such an economic system capable of the necessary level of industrialization and manufacturing in countries which now produce mostly agricultural products and raw materials.

These countries have crying needs for all kinds of *trained personnel*. Many of them have no more than a small handful of doctors, skilled administrators, economists, bankers, entrepreneurs, scientists, teachers, and other professional people. Clearly, many more such people are desperately needed if these complex, though underdeveloped, societies are to function. Perhaps even more urgent, however, is the need for more humble talent, such as better-trained farmers, clerks, plumbers, electricians, mechanics, and even "common" laborers, whose considerable skills and industriousness (so much taken for granted in the industrialized countries) are not at all common in the Third World.

Among the numerous *organizations* needed, the most important is an effective central government to provide basic infrastructure needs, such as transportation and communications networks, power supplies, and school systems, as well as to preserve the order necessary for the economy to function smoothly. But other organizations are indispensable, too. They must provide banking, credit, and insurance facilities; mechanisms for processing, storing, distributing, and marketing agricultural and manufactured products; informational and educational concerns to publish books, periodicals, and newspapers, as well as run broadcasting facilities; and professional associations, labor unions, and farm groups. Most of these organizations, public or private, are either nonexistent or primitive in much of the Third World, in part because of the scarcity of trained personnel to create and manage them, in part because of widespread resistance to changing the old way of doing things, and in part because many of these institutions are associated with Western capitalism—which is widely regarded as responsible for the exploitation of the colonial era. Economic progress probably requires that these barriers to the development of modern economic organizations be overcome.

Many of the countries of the Third World are rich in *natural resources*. Many have ample arable land and water, as well as good climates for agricultural production; and some have enormous timber or mineral or oil reserves. A few, such as Brazil, Zaire, India, and Indonesia, are rich in a number of these basic natural resources. And some, notably the oil-producing countries, have been able to use these resources to begin to overcome some of the problems of underdevelopment. Others, the poorest of the poor countries, are devoid of virtually any naturally endowed resource.

The most often-cited scarce resource in the Third World is finance capital with which to exploit the natural resources and to employ the manpower. Since domestic capital arises from the excess of production over consumption, one of the most serious obstacles to the accumulation of capital to be invested in industrial growth is the insistent fact that the Third World's people must consume virtually all they produce just to survive.

To a pitifully limited extent the capital deficiencies in the Third World have been alleviated by foreign investment, loans, and foreign aid from the world's wealthier countries. The principal source of foreign-exchange export earnings has been limited by the falling price of Third World primary-product exports, the need to import foodstuffs to feed the population, and the increasing interest charges on loaned capital. But substantial increases in domestic savings are not likely as long as most of the burgeoning populations in these countries continue to live so close to the subsistence level.

Perhaps the most important, though often overlooked, requisite for even modest economic development is the widespread popular acceptance of a *supportive doctrine* or set of attitudes that values the virtues of work, production, sacrifice, saving, growth, pragmatic approaches, and optimism; and insists upon the almost moral necessity of striving toward these goals. Only as substantial numbers of people adopt these attitudes can their societies remedy the otherwise crippling shortages of entrepreneurs, skilled and productive workers, and surplus capital for investment. The industrialized countries of the world all possess some variant of this dynamic élan. On the other hand most of the underdevelopment countries do not. There one frequently finds, instead, a mixture of fatalistic skepticism and even antipathy toward these values. Skepticism suggests that change and progress are unlikely, that struggling to overcome poverty is futile; this attitude, with historic and cultural roots, may also be sensible and realistic, given existing limited economic opportunity for Third World people. The antipathy, often with religious roots, sometimes suggests that materialism, materialistic goals, and materialistic activities and occupations are odious; or it may suggest, following Gandhi or the Islamic leaders of Iran, that these values and goals are corrupt Western outlooks foisted off on helpless subject peoples just as Western political institutions were. Whatever the reason, whether fatalism or antagonism, these old traditional beliefs die very slowly; and as long as they retain their potency, they impede the industrialization required for economic development.

Thus, much of the poverty gripping the underdeveloped world must be attributed to the circumstances prevalent there, to local conditions and forces in the poor countries themselves.

The International Dimension

But the relationship between the rich countries and the poor countries contributes to and aggravates the poverty of the underdeveloped world; and many of the policies and actions of the wealthy countries and financial institutions of the North have perpetuated the difficulties of the South. Though freed from their former colonial status, these poor countries remain trapped in a continuing dependency relationship, playing a subordinate role in the global economic system created and controlled by Northern governments and powerful multinational corporations to serve their own interests. During the colonial era most of these poor countries were restricted by their foreign rulers to the production of raw materials to feed Europe's industrial needs. As a result, Third World countries found themselves in the twentieth century in a position of receiving a much smaller share of world wealth than the metropolitan countries after having provided the raw materials, often through slave labor, for the industrialization of the latter.

These poor countries still depend for their support earnings on the sale of these few basic commodities or raw materials to the wealthy, industrialized North. The prices of these commodities (tea, copper, oil, sugar, rubber, jute, bananas, etc.) have been very much controlled in the North, have fluctuated unpredictably, and have not kept pace with the prices of manufactured imports. (The Jeep that Columbia could import in 1950 for 17 bales of coffee, for example, cost 67 bales in 1965 and over 200 bales in 1980.) Static or falling commodity prices prompt the poor country to increase production to boost sales; but this emphasis on commodity production for export results in the diversion of energy, land, fertilizers, and workers away from domestic food production with consequent malnutrition and starvation. Rich countries, meanwhile, work to minimize the prices of the commodities they import: they subsidize their own farms and mines, they erect trade barriers to foreign imports, they develop alternatives or synthetic substitutes for once-imported materials (plastics to reduce demand for rubber or copper, for example), and they drag their feet in response to proposals made by the poor countries for stabilizing commodity prices, increasing commodity prices, or otherwise improving the terms of trade for the poor countries.

Poor countries that attempt to extricate themselves from this exploitative subservience by initiating industrialization soon find that they must borrow needed capital from banks, corporations, and other credit structures controlled by the rich in the North, thus taking on frequently crushing burdens of debt and inevitably finding themselves once again manipulated dependents of their bankers and creditors. And they also must become dependent upon Northern technology, educational and training institutions, technicians, and spare parts for their industrialization projects.

Moreover, much of the most productive land and most valuable resources of the Third World remained in the hands of foreigners after political independence. One effect of this foreign ownership has been to remove control of the most important sectors of the economy from people in the country and thus to subject the growth and direction of the economy to external forces. Not only does this mean that basic elements of a development policy (investment, employment, inflation, etc.) are not really within the control of the national government, but that these decisions are likely to be taken on the basis of interests other than those of the developing country. Economic development is thus conditioned and constrained by external forces.

After all this, the poor countries of the Third World often find that their manufactured products are either kept out of Northern markets or fetch low prices there, because the governments of rich countries have adopted tariff policies and subsidies to protect their own manufacturers.

Although, as we have pointed out, this dependency has roots in the colonial past, in contemporary times one of the most important links through which it is maintained is the transnational enterprise (TNE). The transnational enterprise is a large corporation which, although its corporate headquarters are in one country, has worldwide operations and is engaged in business in a number of different countries. It may be involved in the extractive sector (Shell, Alcan), the commercial sector (Sears, Bata Shoe), food (W. R. Grace, General Foods), services (ITT, Trust Houses Forte), or a conglomerate including all of these (Gulf/Western). The different activities of the TNE are located in different countries and thus the overall operation escapes the scrutiny and control of any one government. With the activities of the TNE being geared to benefit the larger corporation rather than any of its national operations and certainly not primarily the national interest of host countries, the lack of control by the host country makes it difficult to assure that this kind of investment contributes to development.

In the 1950s and 1960s the TNE was optimistically looked to as one of the principal mechanisms for bringing wealth and well-being to the impoverished masses of the Third World, and even today a glance at their public relations releases and annual reports indicates that they still present themselves in this light. In fact, the impressive growth rates experienced by some developing countries during the 1960s was no doubt due in some measure to the direct foreign investment of TNEs. By the 1970s, however, some of the countries which had received large doses of this direct foreign investment were realizing that this growth was not synonymous with development, and that the benefits were indeed very limited. The contribution to the net capital of the developing country was often small, because the TNE would often borrow locally, thus depriving indigenous entrepreneurs of a share of scarce financial capital. The creation of new jobs was also limited as production techniques were based on the labor-saving devices designed to lower costs in the home country, where capital was relatively more abundant and thus cheaper than labor. Those individuals who did find employment with the TNE were well paid, often enjoying wages far higher than their equivalents in local enterprises. These high wages paid to a relatively small elite of the work force had the dual effect of concentrating the increased income in the hands of a few people with a high propensity to import, thus reducing the stimulus to the local economy, and of pushing up wage demands in the local sector, reducing the ability of this sector to compete and contributing to inflation.

The poorer countries of the Third World also forfeited potential revenues by offering 25 or 30 year "tax holidays" as an inducement for foreign investment, long periods when the investing firm is exempt from local taxation. It is not difficult to see how a number of host countries have come to consider the TNE as a negative element in the development process; and recent empirical studies have shown that in many cases this form of "investment" has resulted in a net transfer of capital from the developing country to the investing country. Further negative social and political effects of the activities of the TNEs have included the dissemination of tastes of the high-level consumer society for imported luxury goods at the expense of local tastes, and intervention in the local political process through bribery and direct political action to destabilize the existing order. All of these considerations have led to a re-assessment of the role of direct foreign investment in development and made the TNE one of the most controversial institutions in international relations.

The rich countries of the North, with superior power and bargaining strength, have sought and continue to seek to maintain this unequal status quo, to remain dominant, to reap the economic benefits of a one-sided international system. Perhaps this is understandable. But at the same time this network of relationships, policies, and actions contributes to the continuing and deepening impoverishment of the underdeveloped world and aggravates the explosive situation in the southern hemisphere, where three-fourths of humanity lives.

Inadequate economic performance and underdevelopment inevitably result in mass dissatisfaction, which focuses ultimately on the vulnerable political system. Expectations have been frequently raised unrealistically high by some recent modest improvements, by politicians' promises, by people's observing the standard of living enjoyed by the wealthy elites of their own societies, and by seductive media portrayals of allegedly appropriate goals. Expectations become demands on the economic and political machinery that is usually weak, giving rise to frustration and outrage. And while fatalism and stoic acquiescence may persist generally among the populations, there are enough of the outraged who have shed these constraints on political action to threaten public order and even whole political systems. A fair amount of chronic Third World instability, thus, has economic roots.

Challenge to Order

This chronic instability—due to these factors of festering regional conflicts, abject poverty, the population explosion, internal weaknesses common to most underdeveloped countries, and the web of inequitable North–South links—might not have threatened global peace in an earlier time. The strong, wealthy states of the world might have been safely able to ignore such quarrels and poverty far beyond their own shores. These far off lands could simply be left to "stew in their own juices," so to speak, without endangering their distant neighbors in more fortunate lands.

Today, however, these problems are not so easily ignored; and the instability of the Third World is of grave concern to the world as a whole. This concern is grave not because the "have" nations are becoming so much more humanitarian and charitable that they are deeply troubled by the plight of the huddled masses in the "have-not" nations, though there does seem to have been some slight increase in these noble sentiments over the last few centuries. Rather, it is grave because disorder in the Third World today endangers world peace; and we are better at acting out of fear than we are at responding to our humanitarian instincts. It is now simply quite clear that comfortable peoples can no longer safely ignore the untidy Third World.

But the concern is not, as some writers suggest, a fear that somehow the billions of impoverished colored people of the poor continents will soon, or ever, take up arms and march into a great race-class conflict with the less numerous, wealthy

Caucasians of Europe and North America. This alarmist contingency is virtually inconceivable. Not only would overwhelming technical and military obstacles block such a crusade, but so also would the obvious disunity of the Third World. Despite widely shared anticolonial sentiments that have a racial component, and despite occasional attempts, by the Chinese among others, to develop Third World racial and class solidarity, there are just too many firmly rooted antagonisms blocking such a bizarre confrontation.

In fact, most of the nations of the Third World, despite their anticolonial fulminations, are anxious for good and profitable relations with their wealthy developed neighbors. Latin American governments seek United States friendship, aid, trade, and tourism. Many former British and French colonies in Africa and Asia chose to remain in the Commonwealth or French Community to reap the economic and political benefits. And several times when disruption has threatened to topple a government or destroy a fragile state, the beleaguered regime has even called for military assistance from the former colonial *metropole*. Tanganyika (later united with Zanzibar and renamed Tanzania) and Cyprus, as examples, both sought British troops for emergencies in late 1963, and the following year Gabon asked France for military aid to suppress an attempted military coup d'état. So it is not an impending war of developed against undeveloped or colored against white that is on the minds of worried world leaders.

Instead, they fear that the domestic turmoil and localized clashes may themselves get out of hand, either by spilling out and spreading beyond their obvious confines, or by sucking the superpowers into a clash that could result in thermonuclear war. The first danger results largely from technological advances in weaponry; the second danger is a result of the Third World's frequently becoming an arena for playing out cold-war competitions.

Technological advances and scientific "progress" mean that the Third World countries increasingly have sophisticated weapons at their disposal for use in suppressing domestic disorder, as well as waging war against neighboring states. Airplanes, short-range missiles, armored vehicles, communications equipment, and mass standing armies all make possible in the underdeveloped world the kind of large-scale, mechanized violence so much more difficult to contain than the nineteenth-century tribal wars fought in the Third World with spears and elephants. Furthermore, many of these countries could quite easily and in the very near future develop nuclear weapons. Israel, Egypt, South Africa, Pakistan, Brazil, and Argentina could follow India and China, also underdeveloped, into the nuclear club. And since these countries are not 8,000 miles away from their respective immediate adversaries, and since these adversaries do not possess sophisticated warning and defensive capabilities against air attack, the Third World countries would not need the elaborate and expensive bombers and missiles that the United States and the Soviet Union must have to deliver their warheads; a simpler and cheaper delivery system would do. Perhaps even more frightening is the prospect that these nations will decide instead to develop chemical and biological warfare capabilities which are potentially as potent as nuclear weaponry and have the additional appeals of being cheaper and easier to develop secretly. Modern warfare between Third World states—whether waged conventionally, with nuclear weapons, or with exotic germs—would quite clearly endanger surrounding areas, and might even escalate out of hand to threaten world security. If Egypt and Israel, for example, were ever to wage nuclear or biological warfare against each other, the environmental poisoning alone would be a severe threat to people in far-off spots on the globe. So technological refinements provide one reason why Third World instability can no longer be safely ignored.

The second reason is that the Third World has become entangled in the East–West struggle, with the superpowers and their associates intervening politically, economically, and even militarily in Third World affairs (see Figure 3.4). As the balance of terror stalemated the East–West struggle in Europe, the superpower adversaries shifted some of their energies into a competition, still going on vigorously as we enter the 1980s, for converts, followers, United Nations votes, economic advantages, influence, and psychological victories in the Third World.

This rivalry has drawn the superpowers into some Third World quarrels on opposite sides, as in the Middle East, where the United States is generally sympathetic to Israel's case while the Soviet Union supports the Arab states. Or the two superpowers sometimes find themselves on opposite sides in a civil conflict such as the Vietnam War or the Congo's disorders of the early 1960s. Most dangerously, all the industrialized countries sell and give arms to the Third World, partly for the profits to be made, partly to stabilize precarious regional military imbalances, partly also as an aspect of the cold-war competition. The United States is the world's largest seller of arms to the Third World, trailed by the Soviet Union, France, and Great Britain, in that order. To some extent, no doubt, the arms promote peace by preserving military balances between such feuding

Figure 3.4 The Importers' and Exporters' Shares of Major-Weapon Supplies to the Third World, 1970–1979.

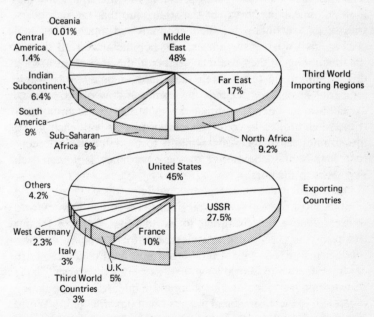

Source: (Stockholm International Peace Research Institute, *World Armaments and Disarmaments: SIPRI Yearbook:* 1980, p. 62.)

countries as India and Pakistan, or Israel and Saudi Arabia, or Brazil and Argentina; but the usual consequences of these arms sales are to exacerbate tense situations, impoverish unstable nations that ought to be spending precious resources on development rather than on unproductive military hardware, and increase the likelihood of superpower clash if armed conflict erupts between client states. Economic assistance to the underdeveloped nations is useful, even indispensable; but superpower cooperation would be preferable to the present rivalry, which often precipitates confrontation. At any rate, the problems of the Third World are clearly sources of global tensions, partly because they can all too easily trigger superpower confrontations, with the danger of thermonuclear holocaust always ominously in the background.

Finally, of course, the wealthy countries of the world are eager to minimize instability in the Third World so as not to endanger their sources of indispensable raw materials; any turmoil and instability threatens the status quo that the rich countries seek to maintain for their economic advantage. Regional clashes, civil wars, insurgencies, and popular unrest all disrupt the functioning of the economic sectors in the area of instability; this disruption, in turn, is felt thousands of miles away where industrial machinery depends on a smooth flow of oil, copper, agricultural products, and other raw materials. If the poor countries are embroiled in conflicts domestically or with each other, they cannot make their contribution to the international economy that is of such interest to the governments of their rich neighbors to the north.

As a source of present global tensions, then, Third World troubles rival the East–West dispute. Perhaps the Third World is even a more serious threat to world order, because the intensity of the East–West struggle seems to be waning and improvements in U.S.–USSR relations are at least conceivable. In contrast, the Third World's agonies, as we have suggested, may be worsening; regional disputes are more intense, the population explosion is increasing, and internal stability for Third World states seems further off in many cases than it did ten years ago. While the East–West struggle may be easing, the afflictions of the Third World, carrying with them threats to international peace, seem to be just beginning. As the East–West struggle replaced the Balkans, perhaps the Third World will replace the East–West struggle as the central worry for this generation and the next generation of world leaders and scholars.

The Global Ecological Crisis

Transcending the two great schisms of East and West and North and South is a problem facing humanity—a problem which is more profound and subtle in its complexity and pervasive scope and at the same time usually manifested in the most mundane and common ways. Yet the potential impact of this global crisis on contemporary and future civilization is as devastating as the possibility of a major thermonuclear war or the squalor prevailing in parts of the Third World. It has been triggered by the ever-increasing depletion and often wanton destruction of the natural resources and the very environment upon which civilization and humanity depend for survival itself.

The origins of this global crisis are lost in the prehistoric roots of mankind when humans began the ever-continuing quest to master nature and use it for their own ends. Kenneth Boulding, in his book *The Meaning of the Twentieth Century,* sees the contemporary crisis as leading us into a second great transition equal to that from precivilized society. Dennis Pirages, who takes as the title to his book, *Global Ecopolitics,* a term that characterizes this crisis, compares the approaching transition in magnitude to two earlier historical watersheds: the agricultural revolution and the Industrial Revolution. He insists that the recent extended period of rapid economic growth and expansion is now being brought to a close by the "new scarcity" of once-abundant, over-exploited, and increasingly expensive natural resources, and that we are being impelled into a "postindustrial" world of more limited opportunities, which will require the development of an entirely different world view if humanity is to make the transition relatively smoothly.

Let us examine the roots of this situation in which we find ourselves.

The human race has always had to contend with environmental limits to the growth of its population, as does any biological population. As long as human beings made their living as the other animals do—by simple hunting and gathering—they were constrained by competition with other species for food and by the limits of what supplies nature provided. Their growth and expansion was quite slow, reaching a population of only about 5 or 10 million persons over a period of more than 100,000 years (perhaps as much as 3 million years for the genus *Homo*).

From the advent of the agricultural revolution, between 8,000 and 9,000 B.C., the development of the human race has been characterized by much more rapid growth and expansion: in a 10,000 year period, our numbers doubled six or seven times to about 500 million. With the cultivation of plants and the domestication of animals came the settling of populations into relatively permanent communities with resultant social and political changes whose impacts are still manifest today. As groups evolved from nomadic to sedentary societies, food supplies became more secure, populations grew, and this gave birth to the territorial community which was the precursor of the modern nation-state. Increased food production provided a surplus, which freed a portion of the population to specialize in other activities, such as religion, artifact production, politics, and warfare.

The Industrial Revolution, which began to gather momentum in the fifteenth and sixteenth centuries A.D., continued our progress toward the conquest of nature and the pushing back of her limits upon us by providing another great leap in productivity through the use of machinery which harnessed the energy of cheap and abundant fossil fuels: coal, and more recently, petroleum and natural gas. In the present stage of the Industrial Revolution, fission, the harnessing of the forces which bind the atom, is seen by some as the new hope for a further energy source; and research is continuing toward the development of the use of fusion, the process which drives the sun itself. But even with our present rapidly advancing technology, these two processes may never be able to provide energy cheaply enough to continue to foster our seemingly unlimited growth. In the past 300 years the human population has increased from 500 million (half a billion) to over 4 billion, and is expected to double in the next 40 years, even by conservative estimates (it will triple by then if birth rates remain the same as they are today).

The Industrial Revolution gave rise to a surplus of real wealth and to societies that were capable of supporting large armies and providing them with sophisticated weaponry. It created huge industrial complexes in the rapidly developing parts of the world, which used those armies to conquer and exploit vast colonial empires. The colonies provided the necessary inexpensive and plentiful raw materials to feed that machine and eventually provided further markets for its products. Thus this system of large-scale exploitation of many nonrenewable natural resources produced an abundance that is the direct cause of the exponential population and consumption explosion of the past 300 years, as well as colonialism, two world wars, and the present international system.

It is perhaps a fundamental characteristic of human nature to be unable to perceive events beyond the most urgent contemporary problems, and the two major international schisms have provided serious challenges to our ability to cope with them. Recently, however, concerned persons have become acutely aware of the immediacy of the overriding problem posed by the growth and expansion of humanity and consumption to the point where mankind faces an imminent transition of a magnitude equal to that of the agricultural or industrial revolutions. This transition will derive from the fact that civilization, as it is presently evolving, is rapidly approaching the limits of the earth's environment to support it. The nature and scope of this crisis are unprecedented; and present-day institutions and dominant philosophies are inadequate to see us through it. The first two transitions were largely fortuitous: they "happened," the human race was not pushed into them. But the present transition is inescapable. As we approach the limits of our environment's "carrying capacity," we must adapt our world views and social institutions, our values and survival rules, or face the age-old population control of starvation, with the subsequent disastrous disruption of present human social institutions. We may plan our transition into the postindustrial world to proceed with a minimum of such disastrous disruption, or we may go on as we have, ignoring the need to change . . . and the change will come haphazardly and catastrophically.

The struggle for human survival on this planet is a problem that has truly global dimensions. Overpopulation is not just a problem for India, China, or Haiti; pollution is not just a problem for the United States, Western Europe, or Japan. In fact, these are global problems which pose worldwide threats, but which are thus far unfortunately perceived by too many only in their most superficial local manifestations. If we are to survive, we must cast off the present prevailing world view that we are dominant over nature and can continue our recent economic and population growth indefinitely, while maintaining the standard of living all humanity would like to achieve. It would be soothing to believe that science will somehow "save us." But to try to build a world on such hopes or beliefs is to court disaster. The past growth of technology is no guarantee of continuing miracles in the future. If we can just barely support 4 billion people with today's profligate use of finite fossil fuels and petrochemicals, how will we support 6 or 8 or 12 billion people when those resources are gone? We may discover some substitutes for our current fuels, fertilizers, and drugs; but it is unwise to stake human life on very many hoped-for miracles.

An abundance of resources in relation to demands permits the growth of population and of higher levels of consumption; we must learn to acknowledge the converse and intelligently plan how to cope with it. The direction for students of international relations seems clear: global problems of short resource supply, high energy prices, malnutrition and starvation, inflation, inequities in international trade, recession, human rights issues, and political instability indicate that the international relations of the near future must become more concerned with economic and ecological realities and imperatives. As potential threats to national security become increasingly economic and ecological in nature, control and ethical use of the world's natural resources will soon be the major item determining national political priorities and strengths.

The Limits to Growth

The true nature of the global challenge was brought to the attention of the world most starkly by the publication in 1972 of the Club of Rome's first report, entitled *The Limits to Growth*, and the nearly simultaneous publication of "A Blueprint for Survival" by the editors of *The Ecologist*. In words that the layperson could understand, these statements described the imminent crisis that civilization faces as a result of our quest to conquer and harness nature in our endless pursuit of greater material well-being. In short, modernization—along with its economic counterpart, industrialization—produces effects that have grossly disturbed the inherent self-regulating mechanisms of the world's environment. If growth continues to occur as it has in the past several hundred years, the world ecosystem faces imminent collapse, with catastrophic consequences for the human race and life as we know it.

To reach the predictions published in *The Limits to Growth,* a team of scientists at the Massachusetts Institute of Technology undertook a computer simulation to project the results of the interaction of a complex set of variables under conditions of continued growth; they concluded that this collapse would occur within the next hundred years. Although their gloomy verdict has been criticized on a number of grounds, they succeeded in drawing attention to a crucial truth that previously had been virtually ignored: growth cannot continue indefinitely. A change in the fundamental values toward growth must take place, and the longer this change is delayed, the worse are our chances of averting catastrophe.

The limits to growth are imposed by a large number of different factors interacting in a complex way; but basically they boil down to problems of the size of the human population in relation to the availability, depletion, and destruction of the natural resources upon which this human population depends. The recently published *Global 2000 Report* condenses some of the issues and, while it is difficult to discuss them separately because of the complicated ways in which they interrelate, we might list them primarily as problems of adequacy of food supplies, water, air, energy sources, and nonfuel minerals. It is important to remember that the *Global 2000 Report* projections are based on the assumption that there will be no major global disaster such as world war, economic collapse, or widespread disease epidemics.

Of course, underlying all of these problems of scarce resources is the real culprit: overpopulation. Even though the rate of population growth seems to be slowing slightly, in sheer numbers the population is growing faster and faster because there are 100 million more people born each year to grow up and have babies of their own. Even with continued attempts to slow the rate of growth worldwide, the most conservative estimates predict that world population will climb at least 50 percent by the end of this century, to over 6 billion. And nearly all of that increase will be in the less developed parts of the world which, of course, can least afford to support it. It will put increasing burdens on their already-strained support systems, their impoverished countrysides, their increasingly desperate urban situations. It would seem that there is almost no way to avoid catastrophic starvation and the collapse of social institutions in some of these areas during the early part of the next century.

Starvation is nature's uncaring way of limiting expansive populations, and the limits of world food production in the face of rapidly increasing world population constitute the major check on continued growth. Presently, at least one-third of the people in the world are inadequately nourished, but this is the result of grossly uneven distribution of available food rather than actual worldwide shortages. The overconsumption and waste of food by peoples of the developed countries, as well as poor systems of redistributing surpluses, are the main causes of starvation and malnutrition today. But in just a few years absolute worldwide shortages may make any amelioration through more even distribution impossible, due simply to the lopsided growth of populations in the Third World. This eventuality is predicted in spite of the fact that advanced technology in the areas of fertilizers and genetic research to engineer more highly productive crops is expected to increase world food production nearly 90 percent in the next 20 years. However, the major part of this increase will occur and be mostly used in the developed countries of the world; and this phenomenal-sounding 90 percent increase would still amount to only a 15 percent per capita increase worldwide. In sad fact, in many parts of the world nutrition per capita is projected to be at least 20 percent below the barest minimum requirement for sustaining human physical and intellectual development. For those who do not actually starve to death, the punishment for being born in many areas of Africa or southern Asia will be severely stunted and subnormal bodies and minds. There will be growing pressures for international food assistance. At the same time, food prices are expected to double.

It must be remembered that these grim projections are based on a "best case" assumption that there will be a continuing drop in world birth rates, and that there will be no deterioration in climate and weather patterns, nor any catastrophic losses from epidemics or plagues due to lack of genetic resiliency in new strains of highly productive food crops. However, a more than moderate risk of both these latter possibilities is seen to exist.

The phenomenal production demands on the soils of the world's croplands (upon which we depend for not only most of our food but also for fibers such as cotton and linen, as well as for such raw materials as rubber) is bound to take its toll in accelerated deterioration of the agricultural resource base. Such production is entirely dependent upon energy-intensive measures, use of chemical fertilizers, pesticides, irrigation, and heavy machinery, all of which in turn are dependent on supplies of oil and gas. As those supplies become scarce and more expensive, world food production prospects will become even more grim.

Some of the side effects of these measures to produce high crop yields have been far from beneficial. Increased use of inorganic phosphate and nitrate fertilizers has been shown to destroy natural soil fertility, thus creating an ever-greater dependence on them; and these chemicals run off or leach into water supplies, polluting them so as to make them incapable of supporting animal life, while at the same time producing health problems to both livestock and humans. Synthetic chemical pesticides that pose even more serious health hazards have also become a mainstay of modern agriculture. They have exerted evolutionary pressures to produce strains of insects that are immune to pesticides, while at the same time they have destroyed natural biological control mechanisms by poisoning less-resistant pest predators higher in the food chain, thus ultimately creating a more serious pest problem than existed before.

Thus, if these energy-intensive measures continue, we will continue to see poisoning of the biosphere and serious deterioration of agricultural soils due to loss of organic matter, erosion, desertification, salinization, and alkalinization. We can see the results of the earliest example of abuse by human civilization through intensive cultivation and irrigation of the once fertile but now devastated ecosystem of the Middle East. Presently, an area the size of the state of Maine becomes barren wasteland each year, economically unfeasible to reclaim. The desert areas of the world are expected to increase 20 percent by the year 2000 because of this continuing destruction of agricultural lands, misuse of grasslands, and the razing of fragile tropical rain forests. Concomitantly, 20 percent of all species of life now on earth will disappear as their habitats are destroyed and they are pressured and hunted into extinction. Quite a grim price to pay in order to continue to feed the ever-increasing mass of humanity.

We depend upon the world's grasslands to supply us with all our meat and milk products, with wool and leather for clothing, and even more importantly, to support the draft animals which still constitute the major energy resource (beyond human endeavor) for one-third of the world's peoples today. These grasslands face the same sorts of pressure as croplands, as more and more marginal land is grazed each year in an effort to support larger herds, and as overgrazed land is ruined and converted to desert all over the world. There will be increasing pressures to do away with food animals and to farm these grasslands for more direct food production. The dust bowl experience of the 1930s in the United States points out the foolhardiness of such attempts.

We have increasingly turned to harvesting the oceans, which currently supply 27 percent of the minimum protein requirements for the world's 4 billion people. But the 70 million tons of fish per year which the world fisheries can now produce seems to be near the maximum that we can realistically expect, and even if new methods of aquaculture could increase this yield to 100 million tons per year, the oceans would contribute less to world nutrition than they do today as the world's population continues to expand. Already, catches are dropping off in many once-productive areas due to over-fishing and increasing destruction and pollution of coastal ecosystems, a resource upon which fisheries depend heavily. And we certainly cannot continue to dump our toxic wastes and garbage into the oceans with impunity, for not only does the life in the sea furnish us a valuable food resource, it produces most of the planet's oxygen.

It is ironic in a world, four-fifths of whose surface is covered with water, that lack of water itself should be a sharply limiting factor in our environment. Unfortunately, demands on fresh water supplies are already critical in many parts of the world and population growth alone will cause human water requirements to more than double by the year 2000, without factoring in any increases in standards of living. Much of this projected increase in water use will be for irrigation in the attempts to increase food production. Fresh water diverted in and out of natural watercourses a number of times during its journey to the sea becomes increasingly salty from such use as it returns downstream, becoming eventually unusable. Our rural waters are becoming increasingly polluted from heavy applications of fertilizers, herbicides, and pesticides to surrounding croplands; there is as yet no known way to filter out these dangerous chemicals, many of which do not break down into harmless residues. Urbanized, industrialized areas contribute their own brands of pollution to our water systems as they use water for cooling and sewage purposes. Some of this can be prevented or cleaned up, but only at great economic expense.

And deforestation in the less developed parts of the world will cause water supplies there to become even more erratic.

The only virtually unlimited source of water for human use is the sea, but the use of sea water requires desalinization and transportation of resulting fresh water to needy areas. These processes require immense amounts of energy which will be prohibitively expensive in the years to come.

Although the world's finite fuel resources—coal, oil, gas, uranium—are theoretically sufficient for centuries, we must begin to think ahead toward the day when they will be gone, about how we will support 12 or 20 or even just 4 billion people on this small planet without the energy-intensive approaches now used. For present purposes these energy sources are unevenly distributed over the world; their extraction and use pose serious economic and environmental problems. They are increasingly expensive to obtain, and vary in their amenability to exploitation. The problems of an increasing build-up of extremely hazardous nuclear wastes (with as yet no satisfactory disposal solution), or of air pollution and acid rain (resulting from the production of carbon, sulfur, and nitrogen oxides during the burning of fossil fuels, especially coal) which damage air quality, lakes, soils, crops, and buildings, are serious and must be solved soon if we are not to destroy our environment's ability to support us as we continue to use these resources. And if we are to continue civilization's energy-intensive approach to survival and living, we must search for and find practical new energy sources. Otherwise, civilization as we know it is doomed to extinction when these finite resources are exhausted.

The developed countries of the world today depend predominantly on petroleum as the source of energy which drives their industrial machinery. Oil production is expected to reach maximum capacity by the year 2000. Price increases will require reductions in the standard of living in the industrialized countries; and less developed, poorer nations will be forced to continue to depend heavily on firewood to supply most of their domestic energy. (Today about 90 percent of the wood used in the Third World is burned for cooking and heating.) This presents an extremely serious but virtually ignored problem: By the year 2000, some 40 percent of the world's current forests will be gone, and needs for fuel woods will exceed available supplies by 25 percent. By 2020 all physically accessible forests in the less developed countries are expected to have been completely cut. These predictions take into account anticipated efforts at reforestation. But much of the denudation will involve vast reaches of tropical forests, and when these are disturbed by extensive cutting, the precarious balance of fragile tropical soils, soil nutrients, local temperatures, and rainfall patterns are also disturbed, with the result that neither trees nor grasses (nor, of course, other crops) will naturally grow there again.

As we continue to obtain our energy from combustible fuels, especially coal, we can expect the quality of our air to worsen. This affects our quality of life in several ways more serious than just the obvious dangers inherent in the breathing of polluted air. As already mentioned, the sulfur and nitrogen oxides released in combustion combine with water vapor in the upper atmosphere to produce acid rain, with its resultant damage to lakes, croplands, forests, wildlife, and human structures (particularly buildings made of marble, limestone, or metal). There is also the danger of depletion of the protective ozone layer in the earth's atmosphere, which would permit increases in ultraviolet and other cosmic radiation reaching the planet's surface, which in turn would cause increases in skin cancers, genetic damage, and serious damage to food crops.

Perhaps the most grave consequence of air pollution, though certainly not yet taken seriously enough, is the steadily rising quantity of carbon dioxide in the world's atmosphere. There are conflicting opinions on exactly what effects this will have, but virtual agreement that it will affect the earth's climate to some significant degree in the next few decades. It is now known for certain that the global climate has vacillated widely from warm to cold, wet to dry, in the recent and distant past; that the last hundred years have offered the human race the most favorable period in thousands of years for food production in the temperate zones now occupied by the industrialized nations; and that only a 4 degree annual decrease in world average temperatures is sufficient to cause a major glacial advance. Whether world climate changes provide increased or decreased temperatures and rainfall, any change is apt to seriously affect the ability of the current temperate zone's breadbaskets to feed the world, causing global famine and the death of hundreds of millions of people barely surviving on today's and projected increased food yields. Thus, something as seemingly simple as air pollution could have a massive destructive effect on our future in a variety of ways.

So it is clear that the Industrial Revolution, which promised humanity so much in terms of relief from back-breaking labor and grinding poverty, has resulted as well in the pollution of the environment, ultimately making it a far less hospitable place for human habitation. Chemicals and chemical wastes that cause cancer and genetic mutations are prevalent in industrialized countries, as are many other toxic substances, among them the terribly poisonous heavy metals such as lead and mercury, the effects of which are cumulative and irreversible.

Not only has industrialization seriously threatened the environment through such destructive pollution, but these same processes are hastening the day when they must cease producing the things which provide the wealthy nations with their luxurious standard of living. The natural resources which feed their voracious industrial machines are being consumed at a rate which will deplete them in a matter of decades (see Figure 3.5). Fossil fuels, which took millions of years to create by natural processes, and industrial nonfuel minerals, which exist in finite amounts in the earth's crust, are being depleted at a geometrically increasing rate. Demand for nonfuel minerals will double by the year 2000. Already many of these mineral resources are becoming scarce, and soaring production costs (again, largely a function of energy costs) will put many of the resultant products beyond the reach of all but the extremely wealthy. Even now one-quarter of the world's population uses three-fourths of the world's mineral production. The amount of metal being consumed by each generation is roughly equal to all the metal consumed by all previous generations. While the precise time when each of these vital elements will be exhausted is impossible to predict, the supply is not infinite and this fact imposes the harsh truth that unlimited growth cannot continue indefinitely, and probably not for very much longer.

It is very important to remember through all of this that pollution and depletion are problems for not only the industrialized nations, and that the problem of overpopulation is not

Figure 3.5 U.S. Mineral Consumption.

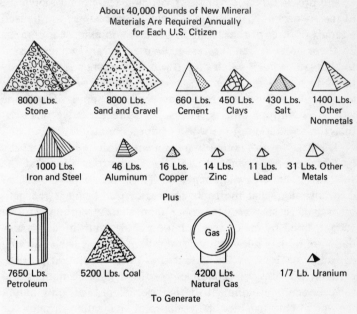

About 40,000 Pounds of New Mineral
Materials Are Required Annually
for Each U.S. Citizen

8000 Lbs. Stone 8000 Lbs. Sand and Gravel 660 Lbs. Cement 450 Lbs. Clays 430 Lbs. Salt 1400 Lbs. Other Nonmetals

1000 Lbs. Iron and Steel 46 Lbs. Aluminum 16 Lbs. Copper 14 Lbs. Zinc 11 Lbs. Lead 31 Lbs. Other Metals

Plus

7650 Lbs. Petroleum 5200 Lbs. Coal 4200 Lbs. Natural Gas 1/7 Lb. Uranium

To Generate

Energy Equivalent to 300 Persons Working Around-the-Clock for Each U.S. Citizen

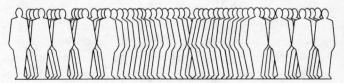

U.S. Total Use of New Mineral Supplies in 1975 Was About
4 Billion Tons

Source: (Gerald O. Barney, ed., *The Global 2000 Report to the President of the United States,* vol. 2. Elmsford, N.Y.: Pergamon Press, 1980, p. 384.)

confined to the Third World. When we view these situations from a global perspective, the affluent societies of the northern hemisphere clearly contribute heavily to the stresses on the environment of this overpopulated planet. The destructive impact of each individual on the global environment is far higher in these countries. The amount of the earth's scarce resources of land, water, minerals, energy, and clean air "used" by an American to produce a one-ton vehicle, pave the roads to carry it, and provide the fuel for transporting a 150-pound individual to the supermarket to obtain the highly processed food to feed a family of three or four living in a twelve-room house is perhaps 25 times greater than the resources used by an Indian peasant to cultivate a small patch of earth to feed a much larger family living in a one- or two-room dwelling. Measured by the pressure it places upon scarce resources, the population of the world's wealthy countries makes far more excessive demands than the population of the world's poorer countries.

The irony of this is that there is a widely shared belief on the part of leaders of wealthy and poorer countries alike that the solution to underdevelopment and Third World poverty is industrialization, that the route to greater well-being is the path of ever-increasing growth rather than sharply curbing growth accompanied by major redistribution efforts and the accommodation of human numbers and aspirations to the earth's carrying capacity. As long as the outdated growth orientation persists, continued desires for economic growth by the rich nations and for economic development by the poorer ones will only hasten the day of catastrophic total collapse of civilization through the depletion and destruction of the environment on which it depends.

This is not to say that Third World nations are "wrong" in their aspirations and attempts to alleviate the poverty and misery of their peoples, simply that they are naive to believe they can follow the same route of economic growth pursued by the developed countries over the last 300 years. These poorer countries are trapped between the inequities of today's distribution of global wealth and the limits to growth imposed by the ecological crisis and resultant scarce and expensive resources. The

Third World countries do not have colonies to exploit in order to fuel their development, as the now wealthy nations had when they began to industrialize. They do not have the option of expanding territorially in order to command a supply of the seemingly limitless resources which were available 200 years ago. Under the conditions of poverty that widely exist in their countries, they have no way of building up a supply of capital to invest in industrialization. They are simply prevented from following in the footsteps of the industrialized North.

The tremendous recent increases in petroleum prices are another reason they cannot follow the energy-intensive path the North took. Most Third World countries import nearly all their energy supplies, except for firewood, and these price increases have tripled and quadrupled their costs of undertaking industrial activities. Their costs have also skyrocketed for the petroleum-based fertilizers upon which they have become dependent in order to wring ever-higher crop yields from their soils. And as importers of finished products, they have had to pay higher prices for their imports, since Northern manufacturers have passed along to consumers the extra costs of manufacturing caused by increased energy prices.

There are no easy answers for the Third World. The situation is extremely complex and demands complex, multiple answers. The industrialized world must provide food assistance and support higher prices for resources and goods imported from their poorer brothers until these nations can get on their feet. And these nations might also take a lesson from the success of labor-intensive methods and the less complex, more modest *appropriate technology* employed by China in its heroic effort to pull itself up with a minimum both of outside help and of expensive, energy-intensive, *high technology,* which poses such perils to the global environment. China also provides possible lessons in controlling population rate increases. The largest nation in the world numerically, China hopes to reach zero population growth by the year 2000, less than 40 years after beginning its population-control program.

What is desperately needed now for rich and poor nations alike is a radical change in our world view of ourselves as dominant over and in control of nature. We must learn to see the human race as a biological entity existing in a very fragile biosphere, the composing ecosystems of which we cannot continue to abuse with impunity. Our commitment to ever-increasing growth and overconsumption underlies the present ecological crisis and approaching ecological disaster. Because biological resources are renewable does not mean they are indestructible. They are presently shrinking along with nonrenewable minerals and fuels, and once these are gone, through depletion or destruction, it will be too late to start conserving and managing for the long term. We must determine the carrying capacity of our global environment, recognizing the natural law that a biological population of any species will expand to fill its available resource space, or *niche,* and will be limited by the resource in shortest supply. Trade can expand this natural carrying capacity, but to permit population expansion very far beyond the support capabilities of local supply limits is to become very vulnerable to external political manipulation and to court catastrophe if the external supplies are cut off because of international politics or changing natural conditions such as climate or epidemics. We must alter the current suicidal relationship between ourselves and the earth's natural systems and resources. We must make important viable decisions that will determine what and how much we eat, how we live, and how many children we have. And we must leave ourselves a margin of safety.

When the earth's carrying capacity is exceeded, disaster and collapse must surely and swiftly follow. Overconsumption will ultimately force change upon us with catastrophic consequences. Far better that we should begin now to plan for more orderly accommodation of human numbers and aspirations to the capacity of the planet to support us. Social change has traditionally been slow. Even planned, any pervasive and rapid change will doubtless cause great cultural stress and social upheaval. But time is short and the alternative far worse. We must shake loose from the concept of growth and expanding production as a guideline for our social order. We must accommodate ourselves to the earth's carrying capacity, either sensibly and cooperatively with foresight and planning, or be cruelly forced by natural laws beyond our control. If we continue to foolishly believe that we are in control, that catastrophe cannot happen to us, that somehow something will turn up to rescue us while we go on with business as usual, we are surely doomed as a species.

The future may not be so grim if we are able to implement the proper choices soon enough. It is obvious that awareness of this global crisis and impending disaster is spreading. The required new world view based on the recognition of the finite nature of this small planet and the inextricable interdependence of the states and peoples upon it is struggling to establish itself in place of outdated concepts of the human race's dominance and natural right to destroy the world. We already see the development of the necessary new set of values, ethics, and survival rules: the beginning of the shift to renewable energy sources and the decentralization of economic activity; a back-to-the-land move in many industrialized nations; the philosophical differentiation between basic and contrived needs; the conservation ethic and the appropriate technology movement; the notion of "bigger is better" giving way to the concept that "small is beautiful"; the shift toward focusing on improving the quality of life rather than on increasing the quantity of material things owned. There are economic and social policies being developed for encouraging smaller and discouraging larger families all over the world, as many societies struggle to promote population stability as an important goal. We are learning to do more with less technologically. We are developing new ways of thinking about growth, a maturity which can replace physical growth with intellectual, cultural, and moral development. There are many who realize that an economic system that must create new material "needs" through advertising and then new products to satisfy those new "needs" is not sustainable indefinitely, nor even morally defensible in these times.

All of these changes point clearly to the fact that the world has stepped over the threshold of the next great transition, the transition to a postindustrial civilization. The basic question remaining is whether the human race can complete the transition quickly enough to avert the disaster that still waits ahead.

This transition will involve many implications for the political sphere. It implies a necessary reform of international order, as well as social reforms in each nation. Industrial nations must scale down their consumption and developing nations must change their patterns of reproduction and development. The marketplace can promote conservation, but rising prices can also result in the extinction or exhaustion of a commodity as the last whale or the last barrel of oil is sold to the highest bidder. Higher prices can encourage farmers to produce more wheat and yet cause starvation because the poor cannot afford to buy that wheat. It is perhaps unfortunate, but probably true that in order to manage the precarious balance required for human survival on this planet, we are going to be faced with wider government controls and fewer personal freedoms to do the destructive things we have become accustomed to doing.

Such global ecological threats as mineral depletion, desertification, oceanic pollution, and over-fishing can only be managed through international cooperation and planning, the creation of new global approaches and institutions. At the same time, it must be recognized that local dependence on local resources (as far as possible) lessens the vulnerability to natural or political disaster which exists when most of the world depends on one geographic region for food or on another for its fuels. Because national security depends more and more on international economic stability, and because political power now derives more and more from economic rather than military power, governments must become more cooperative and globally concerned, more willing to divert funds and efforts from swords into plowshares.

What is at stake here is no petty national or personal pride, but the survival of the human species. The impending global crisis can be appreciated and dealt with only by means of a holistic perspective that recognizes the delicate and direct connection between individuals and their actions on the one hand, and that of survival on the other. These actions and their consequences are not confined within the territory of a nation, nor are they simply the sum of interactions between governments.

Rather, they transcend such limits to become global phenomena in their own right.

Fundamental individual values lie at the base of an ultimate solution to the ecological crisis. These new values, some of which we have already mentioned, must be reflected in new, more globally oriented institutions and processes for problem solving, which will transcend the present interstate nature of global politics. This is the nature of the challenge to leaders, as well as to all the individual inhabitants of this small planet. Those of us in the industrialized North must perhaps bear more of the responsibility for developing the institutions and processes that will see the world through the great imminent transition, because we have the greatest concentration of wealth and power needed to effect the necessary changes. But will we be willing to move fast enough, to sacrifice some of our luxuries, in order to assure the survival of the endangered biosphere and thus of the human race?

A Dangerous World

We have very briefly sketched three of the more important sources of global tensions: the continuing East–West struggle, the poverty and instability of the underdeveloped world, and the deterioration of the global environment. There are other obvious present threats to world order. For example, nuclear power generation and the spread of nuclear weapons both pose serious dangers. And international financial structures and arrangements seem to many analysts to be perilously fragile. There will doubtless be challenges in the future that we can as yet only dimly envisage. New weaponry breakthroughs and new or revived antagonisms will have to be anticipated and managed. We are told that we may be in the beginning stages of a biological revolution that will affect our institutions and lives as much as the atomic revolution of the last 40 years or even the Industrial Revolution of the last 300 years. If this revolution is pending, we can anticipate profound change and a whole set of problems to worry about. Even today's problems are enormous, complex, and frustrating. In many cases they seem to be insoluble; often the best we can do is to contain or postpone the explosion and hope for gradual improvement. Tomorrow's problems promise to be both more acute and harder to manage, let alone to resolve.

Three final conclusions or impressions emerge from what has been explored. First, it should be quite clear by now that the world's awesome problems are aggravated to the extent that they are dealt with passionately and emotionally, to the extent that they become transformed into ideological causes. The East–West cleavage, the Third World's problems, and the global environmental decay discussed above would probably be difficult, if not intractable, even were wise people of good will to approach them calmly and patiently. Unfortunately, however, these problems have too often been converted into sharp clashes by emotional believers in particular militant ideologies. More often than not the introduction of deeply felt religious or ideological principles into one of these problems ensures that it will become an unresolvable dilemma. What might have been a resolvable or at least manageable issue becomes a pretext for a passionate crusade. Where pragmatic people might have been able to cope with the problem, dogmatic people usually make the task all but impossible.

Second, science and technology have proven to be at best mixed blessings, perhaps, on balance, even curses. Antagonisms that might in an earlier age have resulted in a minor clash involving hundreds or occasionally thousands of victims are now, thanks to scientific "progress," capable of triggering wholesale catastrophes resulting in hundreds of millions of deaths or casualties. One can also point with considerable justification to medical "advances" as the key explanation for increased infant survival, lengthened life expectancy, and the resultant misery and impending chaos in the Third World. In large measure we have modern technological society to thank for urban crowding, environmental pollution, a hectic and unsatisfying life for many, enormous military-industrial machines, bureaucratic dehumanization, and profound alienation. "Improvements" in communications technology have made possible for the first time the kind of pervasive totalitarianism pictured in Aldous Huxley's

Brave New World and approached by Hitler and Joseph Stalin to extents that Ivan the Terrible and Genghis Khan never dreamed possible. Even in more open Western societies, freedom of thought and action have been subtly eroded and manipulated by nationalized media and by the ever-present conformist pressures of a complex, bureaucratic, technological society. The "affluent" and "modern" society that science and technology have made possible, if not inevitable, is in many ways an impoverished regression. And science and technology have certainly had a largely unfortunate impact on international relations.

Third, and finally, the persistence of the same age-old problems of strife, disorder, and injustice suggests at least the possibility that man himself is seriously flawed. Through the ages people have demonstrated an enormous and apparently unchanging capacity for foolishness, incompetence, arrogance, destructiveness, and hate. At the same time we have revealed serious deficiencies in maturity, imagination, talent, humility, wisdom, and good will. This assessment of human nature seems especially apt in explaining our social and political history. For whereas we have proved expert at *scientific* achievement and making *things,* we have been very poor at *social* achievement and making *institutions.* In contrast to the biblical notion that man was created in God's image, the pages of history and the insights of the behavioral sciences indicate that we are seriously defective: feeble and even often wicked. If the human race is so, then it is logical that our creations, institutions, and behavior would fall far short of perfection. Perhaps, as one scientist has suggested, humans are but a planetary affliction, a malignant growth that has marred the environment for an instant of geological time, but that may bear within themselves the seeds of their own demise . . . a fate that may not be far off.

At the very least, it seems probable that disorder and strife will persist throughout the rest of this century. The brave, and probably naive, exponent of optimism regarding the prospects for improving human nature or eliminating its present unfortunate consequences should bear the burden of proof for this probably untenable position. Skepticism, if not pessimism, is a more appropriate and realistic attitude toward such worthy but unlikely prospects.

This has been a somber, sometimes even alarmist, analysis of the world's present state; but, unfortunately, it is probably also a fairly accurate and realistic picture we have sketched of a most dangerous world.

SUGGESTED READINGS

Barney, Gerald O. *The Global 2000 Report to the President of the U.S.* Elmsford, N.Y.: Pergamon Press, 1980.

Brookfield, Harold. *Interdependent Development.* London: Methuen and Company, 1975.

Brown, Lester R. *The Twenty-Ninth Day.* New York: Norton, 1978.

George, Susan. *How the Other Half Dies.* Harmondsworth, England: Penguin Books, 1975.

Heilbroner, Robert L. *The Great Ascent.* New York: Harper & Row, 1963.

Kennan, George F. *Russia and the West Under Lenin and Stalin.* Boston: Little, Brown, 1960.

Meadows, Donella, et al. *The Limits to Growth.* Washington, D.C.: Potomac Associates, 1972.

Mesarovic, Mihajlo, and Eduard Pestel. *Mankind at the Turning Point.* New York: Dutton, 1974.

Myrdal, Gunnar. *Asian Drama.* New York: Pantheon Books, 1968.

Pirages, Dennis. *Global Ecopolitics.* North Scituate, Mass.: Duxbury Press, 1978.

Waltz, Kenneth N. *Man, the State, and War.* New York: Columbia University Press, 1959.

Chapter 4
Problem Management and Conflict Resolution

While the present human condition may be particularly precarious, the world has always been a dangerous place to live. Consequently, humanity has always devoted considerable energy, talent, and resources to coping with these dangers. Over the uneven course of the last few thousand years, we have developed some methods and mechanisms for managing conflict, for reducing the frequency and intensity of armed violence, for restraining overambitious states and statesmen, and for dealing with economic and environmental problems.

In this chapter some of the more important of these methods

and mechanisms will be examined. We will discuss the conflict-management uses and limitations of diplomatic procedures, military techniques, economic and cultural approaches, moral teachings, international law, and international organizations. Though we will briefly discuss how the means under consideration works to promote the goal of order, we also will be concerned with assessing its effectiveness. Our thesis for this chapter can be simply stated: Each of these methods or approaches or mechanisms can often make a useful contribution to world order, but none of them alone is completely reliable, each having serious limitations; in fact, even the whole package is obviously not always enough to prevent or quickly stop the violent conflicts that daily plague us.

Diplomacy

Diplomacy may be defined as the process by which statesmen attempt to attain national objectives through the use of bargaining, negotiations, persuasion, inducements, argument, reason, compromise, and the threat (rather than the actual use) of force. Diplomats, the experts at compromise, are called upon rather than soldiers, the experts at coercion. The diplomats attempt to reach mutually acceptable resolutions of problems so the soldiers either need not be called upon or, if they have already been engaged in battle, can be ordered to lay their arms aside.

If the diplomatic process is successful, the result of all this bargaining is quite often, though not always, some sort of agreement. Simply stated, diplomats make deals. The deal may be an elaborate, formal treaty that will require whatever ratification procedure is called for by each of the signatory states' constitutions. Or the deal may be an unwritten, informal understanding between heads of state—to respect each other's sphere of influence, for example, or to simultaneously implement similar arms-control measures. Usually the elaborate treaties appear more important than they are, while the informal understandings are quite often more important than most treaties. Most treaties deal with rather settled and innocuous matters, often of a technical or commercial nature; presidents and prime ministers can usually safely send such agreements to national legislatures. The informal and unwritten deals between heads of state, on the other hand, very often are kept quiet precisely because they involve significant issues that the government would rather handle inconspicuously.

It should be stressed again that diplomats are national servants responsible first and foremost for advancing their nations' interests. When they go to an international conference or confer privately over lunch with counterparts from other nations, they are attempting to get the best deal for their nations, driving the best bargains they can, conceding little or nothing without return. Their principal obligation is to their government superiors, national objectives, and the national interest—not to order, peace, justice, and brotherhood, except insofar as these objectives are consistent with their nations' foreign-policy goals.

Contemporary diplomacy is really a mixture of traditional or classical procedures and some distinctly twentieth-century additions. Traditional diplomacy was a quiet, continuous process conducted by skilled professionals principally drawn from the aristocratic classes. These urbane gentlemen from the courts of the European states shared a common conservative ideological outlook and a common code of conduct. They made their deals in secret conclaves behind closed doors, away from the glare of publicity and mass public pressures. Wars were begun or prevented or terminated, territory changed hands, bribes and ransoms were negotiated, and marriages were arranged in these usually secret meetings between ambassadors or in secret and polite intergovernmental communiques. The results were announced, but the stages of the bargaining process were not; in secret, the diplomats could more easily make the concessions necessary for mutually acceptable compromise settlements. Much of contemporary diplomacy is still conducted in this traditional way, with shrewd people quietly and patiently working out compromises.

However, a large part of modern diplomacy is conducted publicly, often in large multilateral conferences and frequently via pronouncements carried in the mass media. Often, the aim of such open diplomacy is not so much to arrive at compromise settlements as it is to make ideological propaganda and score debating points for domestic consumption.

The emergence of such open diplomacy in the twentieth century can be attributed to many factors. First, communications advances have made instantaneous international public communications possible; thus governments are able to use mass media for striking righteous postures and enunciating persuasive arguments in the hope that their adversaries will be shamed or pressured by world opinion into making suitable concessions. Moreover, with the chief of state never more than a few minutes away by telephone, there is less reliance on plenipotentiary ambassadors and more immediate control over foreign policy by political superiors back home. Second, transportation advances have made possible dramatic international gatherings (at United Nations headquarters or elsewhere) and colorful summit meetings; few government heads can avoid the temptation of globe trotting in the national interest. Again, the role of the professional diplomat is diminished by these episodic, usually amateurish, forms of diplomacy.

Third, public diplomacy is to some extent a consequence of Western democratic tendencies with the natural resultant pressures for increased popular involvement in government decision making. Public opinion in the Western representative democracies demands and deserves to be kept informed about diplomatic maneuvering. The citizenry is understandably not content to be handed a settlement on a take-it-or-leave-it basis; it insists upon being kept informed of the stages in the process, as well as the final outcome.

Fourth, the new diplomacy can be explained in part as one result of the emergence of two inexperienced, exuberant, at times ideological, usually impatient superpowers on the twentieth-century world stage: the United States and the Soviet Union. Both of these states have tended to view the old Europe —with its dynastic rivalries, petty intrigues, and secret diplomacy—as corrupt and outmoded. Each has often opted for the newer style of public rhetoric, feeling arrogantly confident that history, truth, and justice are on its side; each has felt that public enunciation of its airtight case would produce success without sordid secret covenants. And, routinely, each superpower has viewed the other as corrupt and untrustworthy, a party not to be dealt with if possible and one that cannot be relied upon to keep its bargains; accordingly, each has often clung to the view that evil should be destroyed, not immorally compromised with or vainly trusted.

Fifth and finally, the East–West struggle has been partly ideological; and in an ideological battle for people's minds, propaganda is often more important than tedious bargaining. So a good deal of contemporary diplomacy is conducted in noisy public forums by amateurish, part-time diplomats often more interested in scoring ideological points than in achieving resolutions for difficult and dangerous situations.

Fortunately, it appears that the world's major states are growing increasingly disenchanted with these newer forms of diplomacy and are resorting to the more quiet and productive traditional forms for conducting discussions on the delicate vital question of war and peace. All states continue their platform posturing, but then usually retire to the quiet back rooms for the important, serious negotiations.

How effective is diplomacy as a means of preventing or limiting global conflict? The answer to this crucial question is that diplomacy—old, new, or in combination—is often quite useful in regulating global struggles, but not always. Basically, diplomacy is an effective regulator to the extent that six basic conditions are satisfied:

1. The problem must be one soluble by an agreement.
2. The contesting parties must prefer achieving a settlement for the situation in question to having no settlement at all.
3. The contesting parties must prefer a negotiated deal to a military solution for the situation in question.
4. The contesting parties must all be willing and able to compromise, to accept a settlement that does not fully satisfy any of them.
5. The bargaining must be skillfully conducted by diplomats whose proposals and threats are credible.

6. The negotiated settlement must be acceptable to all the parties.

Many situations will be such that all these conditions will be at least partially satisfied, in which event a negotiated settlement will be possible. If the issues are minor, or vital interests are not at stake, the contestants will prefer diplomacy to military action and will be willing and able to compromise. If the anticipated costs or risks of a military approach are deemed prohibitive, the states will prefer to call on their diplomats rather than on their soldiers. If the power distribution is so one-sided that one state has no choice but to seek an accommodation, diplomatic procedures will probably be used. If the deal worked out has been skillfully designed to reflect power realities accurately, and is reasonably fair and not too punitive, it will have a better chance of acceptance by the parties. Although this seems like a rather formidable collection of "ifs," enough of these limiting conditions are very often sufficiently satisfied that a durable negotiated settlement can be arranged and a conflict avoided or ended.

However, it should be obvious that diplomacy is not a fully dependable method for solving conflicts. All too often one or another of the conditions is not satisfied, with the result that a situation or conflict continues to fester or military procedures are invoked. It should be recognized, in the first place, that a nation might prefer to see the conflict drag on rather than have it ended by diplomatic bargaining. Statesmen frequently feel that their interests would be best served by this tactic, because conflict can provide a useful scapegoat that enables a beleaguered regime (so it hopes) to unify its people and consolidate its power; or the leaders may wish to postpone the bargaining to a later time when their position will be stronger. Second, if the leaders feel that vital national interests are in imminent peril, it may be impossible to reach a compromise agreement. If the very existence and integrity of the state are threatened, leaders find it hard even to envisage, let alone negotiate, a settlement; most leaders at that critical juncture will prefer or be forced by public opinion to resort to military means.

In the extreme emergency, violence and coercion prevail. Third, once military strategy has been resorted to, there are always strong pressures from all sides to fight for a total victory over the enemy, with the idea of a negotiated, compromise settlement becoming virtually unthinkable to the aroused leaders and their emotional constituencies. Fourth, many, maybe most, of the world's present problems are not soluble by negotiated agreement between states. Many of the problems are intractable, perhaps insoluble over the short run. It is difficult to imagine an agreement that would solve the Middle East confrontation between Arabs and Israelis, or the population explosion, or the clash between East and West, or the dangerous fragility of African states and regimes. The best we can hope for from diplomacy in these knotty cases is that the diplomats will be able to smother the fires temporarily. Fifth and finally, the beginning of negotiations does not always mean that coercion will not continue or begin. States have not usually recognized such an either-or choice; rather, diplomatic and military procedures will frequently be under way simultaneously, soldiers fighting on while the diplomats search for a mutually acceptable cease-fire formula. Some of the bloodiest fighting and much of the dying in both the Korean and Vietnamese wars took place after peace negotiations began. For all these reasons, it is necessary to report regretfully that diplomatic procedures are not always reliable panaceas.

In fact, in certain circumstances, diplomacy is or may be destabilizing, or even a dangerous mistake. Some situations are such that the opening of discussions serves only to intensify the passions on either side, fan the smoldering embers, and increase the intransigence displayed by the parties. Discussions between the Peking and Taiwan claimants to rule China, for example, would presumably produce a great outpouring of venom but not positive results at the present time. Likewise, Arab-Israeli talks might be more harmful than helpful at particularly tense times when the best course would probably be an uncommunicative cooling-off period that offered fewer opportunities for dramatic posturing and shrill denunciations.

Moreover, quite often the beginning of diplomatic procedures raises unrealistically high expectations and hopes that are apt to remain unsatisfied as the talks drag on, seemingly fruitlessly and endlessly. The disillusionment that soon sets in leads to frustration and anger which may trigger a renewed and more violent search for military success. Or it may bring on a domestic crisis as the impetuous cast about emotionally for a scapegoat upon whom to fix the blame for diplomacy's failings. People seem to have very little patience with diplomatic bargaining that does not quickly produce positive results. (Curiously, they seem to be more patient with military approaches that are usually no more productive and are slower and greatly more expensive, besides.) It is, then, unwise to risk failure, frustration, and resultant fury by entering into the diplomatic arena at the wrong time with exaggerated expectations. If the circumstances are wrong, diplomacy can lead to dangerous exacerbation of conflict rather than be a helpful antidote.

The diplomatic path may be destabilizing, too, if the outcome of the process is not really mutually acceptable and freely agreed upon by the parties to the discussions. If, instead, the agreement that emerges is imposed on one of the parties and is thus thought to be unfair or punitive, the diplomats may have succeeded only in sowing the seeds for the next round of conflict. They have often been sown when wars terminated with a peace treaty dictated by an excessively punitive victor. Historians generally agree, for instance, that the harsh and humiliating Versailles settlement forced on the Germans at the end of World War I was a major factor in Hitler's rise to power and the subsequent tragedy of World War II. The wrong kind of diplomatic agreement can have dangerous consequences.

The newer forms of open, conference diplomacy are more plagued by these shortcomings and dangers than the older, more quiet diplomacy. Large, multilateral, public conferences at United Nations headquarters or in Paris or Geneva are too often used to propagandize and make speeches filled with righteousness and virility for home consumption; a premium is placed on strident rhetoric rather than serious bargaining. Second, it is more difficult for statesmen to make the necessary concessions and compromises if their constituencies are keeping informed or even watching the debates on television; public proceedings stifle the give-and-take techniques that can only take place privately, offstage. Third, unrealistically high hopes and expectations are more likely to surround a dramatic conclave or exciting summit meeting than a dull, ordinary meeting between faceless, formal diplomats. Hope springs eternal, but more so when presidents get together around a summit table; most such great gatherings are at best disappointing, at worst dangerously frustrating. Fourth, an exciting public gathering of government heads is much less likely than a traditional diplomatic discussion to bring forth a balanced, moderate, and fair settlement for a delicate situation. The glare of publicity, the pressures of time, the passions of public opinion, and the inexperience of government heads will too frequently combine to yield the kind of hasty and unbalanced document that carries the seeds of next year's conflict. Hence, though there is occasionally some virtue in grand conclaves and meetings between heads of state, such twentieth-century innovations in diplomacy are less than invariably successful.

The best diplomacy (usually the most traditional) in just the right circumstances (rare) can, then, be of some help in the constant struggle for order. It is one of our best tools when used properly for the right job. But it is just a tool; like a carpenter's saw, it can get dull, it can be used improperly, it can be used when another tool is more appropriate, it can even be used destructively. In the employ of skilled leaders seeking order, it is a potent instrument; the problem is that we have too few skillful leaders—and some of the skilled are more interested in making or exploiting disorder than in managing it.

The Power Approach

Although diplomacy provides indispensable contacts and communications among the states of the international system, and thus provides a means to discuss, negotiate, and articulate differences in policy motives and objectives, it certainly provides no guarantee that states will not still see force as the best means of attaining their goals once disagreement has become apparent. Yet the international system is not as anarchic as the "state of nature" that Thomas Hobbes described, a constant state of war. War is expected and accepted as the ultimate means of foreign policy, but the history of international relations is not a tale of never-ending war. As was suggested in Chapter 2, the international system by its very being imposes certain limitations on the degree to which states use violence to promote their aims in international politics.

The balance-of-power mechanism of the eighteenth and nineteenth centuries is not operable in the current era. This system requires several states of comparable power to provide a system of constantly offsetting alliances to prevent any single state from dominating the others. The present bipolar distribution of power makes it impossible for the system to operate, especially as the ideological schism compounds the difficulty. The principle of deterrence which underlay the balance-of-power system, however, is still operative in international politics today. This underlying principle of deterrence is to dissuade from the use of violence by presenting the threat of retaliation.

In the nuclear age, successful deterrence is more important than it has ever been before in history. The Soviet Union and the United States each possess the military capabilitiy to destroy each other with thermonuclear weapons. Each is able to set down certain values which cannot be encroached upon without the aggressor running the risk of incurring nuclear attack. Moreover, each is deterred from pre-emptively striking the other with a decisive blow, because each possesses a second-strike capability, the ability to inflict unacceptable damage on the other after suffering an all-out nuclear attack. In earlier historical periods it might have been commonplace to consider war as one of several means of pursuing foreign-policy objectives. Today, with the stakes at the ultimate level, few, if any, objectives can be rationally pursued through the use of nuclear war.

One of the results of this sobering advance in weapons technology has been to make each of the superpowers more aware of the implicit, though clear, rules of the East–West struggle. After 20 years of confrontation both sides are able to discern and learn certain areas of vital interest that are not subject to negotiation according to the traditional diplomatic processes, not negotiable even under the threat of force. This situation, while creating a frightening existence, has resulted in a high degree of restraint on the use of force between the two superpowers.

Through the NATO alliance the United States has made it clear that not only is an attack on the continental United States an offense likely to lead to military retaliation and nuclear war, but any attack by the Soviet Union against another NATO ally will also provoke this response by the United States. On the other hand, the Soviet Union would see United States intervention in Eastern Europe as an encroachment upon Soviet vital interests inviting military response, perhaps nuclear retaliation. In 1962 it was learned in a harrowing manner that the United States considered the emplacement of Soviet missiles in the western hemisphere to be a violation of her vital interests, warranting exercise of the threat of nuclear war.

During the development of the cold war the United States and the Soviet Union have learned quite well that there are distinct modes of conduct that are proscribed by the ultimate possibility of incurring nuclear retaliation. The result of this has been to maintain the cold war between the two great East and West blocs as a truly "cold" war, effectively limiting if not eliminating shooting war as an instrument of policy in the major East–West confrontation. Thus, deterrence seems to have succeeded quite well in keeping a tenuous peace—tenuous because of the catastrophic consequences of its disruption, whether through miscalculation, mechanical failure, or irrational decisions. This peace of deterrence is also subject to disruption by sudden advances in weapons technology which could possibly undermine the delicate stability which has been created.

As we have pointed out, deterrence means the dissuasion of an adversary from attacking by threat of retaliation. Deterrence is effective to the extent that the adversary believes the threat is credible. In the traditional balance-of-power system, an aggressive state was deterred from attempting to dominate or conquer other states by the possibility of other states forming an alliance with the victim to defeat the transgressor. History shows us that deterrence in this period was far from perfect, because states occasionally considered the risk of fighting an opposing alliance a risk worth taking.

So the principle of deterrence is still operative today in the nuclear age. However, the nature of contemporary international politics has changed the nature of the deterrence. Before the major protagonists possessed the capability of completely destroying their adversaries, major war was a rational alternative to consider in pursuing foreign-policy aims. Deterrence was then imperfect insofar as states considered some goals worth the risk of suffering the kinds of sanctions that were likely to occur. As a decentralized means of assuring international peace, deterrence was imperfect.

The effect of today's situation of mutual nuclear deterrence has been to impose a new stability on contemporary international politics. The awesome specter of nuclear war has, so far at least, created an effective deterrent in the main arena of the East–West confrontation. But 35 years is not, after all, a very long time; it is certainly too soon to be sure that, in our nuclear age, deterrence will work indefinitely to stave off the catastrophe. We certainly cannot relax confidently.

In fact, if deterrence is carefully examined, some flaws become so apparent that perhaps we should not relax at all. Most of what we know about both human behavior and government decision making should make us at least skeptical about the soothing picture the confident proponents of deterrence paint.

Deterrence—really a form of applied psychology—is based upon some shaky premises. The people in charge of the buttons in Moscow and Washington (and, increasingly, in other capitals) must at all times behave sensibly. They must value survival more than any other goal. They must be well informed. They must carefully calculate all the consequences and all the pros and cons of each option in every crisis.

These premises seem to some to be historically, psychologically, and politically naive. We know from psychology and history that people can be counted on to behave rationally only part of the time, nonrationally and even irrationally the rest.

Frequently throughout history they have held some things more dear than "mere" survival—honor and glory come to mind. To some extent people are also usually captive of habit or ideology or public opinion. And they may be poorly informed, especially about secrecy-shrouded military capabilities and intentions. They are clearly capable of evil and folly, error and accident, misperception and delusion, incompetence and passion.

The problem may be compounded when such decisions are made by small groups of people rather than by single individuals. What psychologist Irving Janis calls "groupthink" sets in, with all the members of the group so anxious to get along with each other, maintain their power positions, appease the group leader, and push the interests of their respective bureaucracies that they suspend the critical thinking required for rational decision making.

The problem is certainly further aggravated in a crisis situation when time pressures, poorer information, fear, exhaustion, higher risks, and a tendency toward belligerent machismo cause a deterioration in the already low level of rationality we can expect from the flawed mortals hovering over the buttons.

And we know, too, from history and political science that large, complex governments do not always produce sensible policies. Bureaucratic struggles, interagency feuds, budget considerations, public-opinion pressures, imperfect information handling, organizational inertia, and a host of other factors are at work, frequently in the direction of degrading the rationality (or sensibility) of the process.

We are sometimes frustrated by what seems to be less-than-sensible performance by the governments of the Western democracies that we nonetheless regard as superior to authoritarian regimes. Thus, can we really be so confident that the Soviet system will always work as well as it must, producing wise leadership groups that will behave so sensibly throughout the 1980s and beyond, even in the gravest crises? Most of us know too much history to have that kind of confidence in the performance of *any* political system, perhaps especially highly personalistic authoritarian regimes lacking institutionalized controls on executive discretion.

There may be no feasible, workable, and attractive alternative to nuclear deterrence as a mechanism for preventing the mutual suicide that a thermonuclear war would be. But perhaps we ought to regard deterrence as a seriously flawed approach that we are more or less stuck with; much confidence in its long-term efficacy seems unwarranted, more a matter of faith and hope than of well-grounded certainty.

In other parts of the world, particularly in the Third World, the imperfections of deterrence are also apparent. Lacking nuclear weapons, most of the world's countries still try to rely on deterring attacks or accomplishing foreign-policy objectives by increasing their military capability. In the Middle East, the Arab states and Israel have engaged in an arms race which has not succeeded in deterring several outbreaks of war. In India and Pakistan a similar situation has prevailed, with similar results. And the situation is rendered even more dangerous by the support these powers often seek and sometimes get from one or the other of the superpowers. The Soviet Union and the United States, not to mention Great Britain and France, have provided arms materials to other countries of the world not directly involved in the East–West clash, each hoping to maintain the strength of a client state so as to deter attack by its enemies.

It is difficult to assess the degree to which the influx of arms and materials from the sponsor states has contributed to maintaining an equilibrium of forces in the client states and reduced the frequency of war, but it is clear that it has not fully succeeded. Moreover, the situation is rendered more dangerous because the involvement of the superpowers always threatens to turn a minor conflict of the Third World into a cold-war battle with the possibility of escalation into nuclear war. And this possibility would be increased if any of the nuclear powers chose to provide a client state wtih nuclear capability.

Even though possession of strong military forces by a Third World state may provide it with some security against its enemies, quite obviously the problems that these states face are not for the most part problems that can be solved by military force; and the unhappy diversion of scarce resources to develop military strength delays the solution to these problems of underdevelopment. But while the antagonisms that are the heritage of the colonial era still create tensions in the Third World, and so long as they have no other means of assuring security, these states are unlikely to abandon the deterrence principle as a means of assuring some degree of security.

Using force to limit violence in international relations has, then, never been a perfectly reliable approach, because all too often the threat of force has led to the use of violence when the threat failed. This situation will prevail as long as the world remains a decentralized power system with each state free to employ its force violently.

The International-Cooperation Approach

However, it is possible that the degree to which political conflicts and problems are approached through the resort to physical violence can be reduced through the creation of a greater amount of solidarity among the states of international society.

No real commitment to an international community is present in modern international relations. As curious children, we are taught to love and feel loyal to our own countries, our flags, and our institutions rather than to the United Nations, or to our brothers in foreign lands, or to the international community. Our loyalties and commitments are to the national symbols first of all; and when there is a conflict, it is these loyalties that prevail. The international cooperation approach is based on the argument that violence will never be eliminated in international politics and the great problems of the world which we discussed in Chapter 3 will not be solved until social solidarity in the international system is increased.

Advocates of this approach suggest that greater international solidarity can be created by increasing contact and communication among the peoples of the world through such activities among countries as international trade, cultural exchanges, tourism, exchange of students, business contacts, and educational programs. Through economic intercourse, through trade and aid from the developed countries to the underdeveloped, the tensions of the Third World can be alleviated. By the processes of this increased intercourse, the different peoples of the world can come to know and understand each other better. The functionalist argument for international organizations is based upon these premises. The functionalist feels that through cooperation on tasks common to different states and different societies, warlike attitudes and thus warlike behavior will be reduced or eliminated. By learning more about foreign peoples and cultures, individuals will come to realize that people throughout the world are not really so different from each other, are not barbarians or strange creatures to be feared or hated. The basis of this functionalist argument is that wars are the result, either directly or indirectly, of certain objective conditions of humanity. Disease, pestilence, poverty, and ignorance are the roots of war; and once these roots have been extirpated, wars will be eliminated, or at least will occur much less often. Cooperation among states for the purpose of bettering the everyday condition of the human race is thus seen as the way to peace.

It is a fact that modern international society has witnessed a great increase in the number of interactions across state boundaries, and the present foreign policies of many states have included policies that implement some of these ideas. Cultural exchange programs are common today, with the Bolshoi Ballet touring the United States, the Cincinnati Symphony visiting the Middle East, and African dancers entertaining in Europe. Government funds are provided to enable United States students to study in countries throughout the world, and both the United States and the Soviet Union have significant programs for foreign students to study in their universities. Communications satellites allow programs originating in Japan, Mexico, the Soviet Union, or the United States to be beamed throughout the world. The volume of international trade increased significantly during the 1960s and 1970s, and the developed countries instituted regular, if small, programs of foreign aid and assistance to countries of the Third World. Undoubtedly, international intercourse has greatly increased in the past decades.

There is, however, presently no conclusive evidence that such interaction between individuals of different states has increased global solidarity and promoted international peace. First, it is questionable whether greater knowledge of a foreign people and culture improves attitudes and relations. It is possible that greater knowledge may increase fear or hatred; the French and Germans knew each other quite well in 1870, 1914, and 1940, yet they fought bitterly. Second, even though total international intercourse has greatly increased, there is evidence that in comparison to the volume of interactions *within* states there has been no relative increase, and perhaps even a decrease. Third, foreign aid received by an underdeveloped country has often created tension, misunderstanding, and suspicion of neo-colonialism or subversive activity rather than appreciation or understanding between the two countries involved. And finally, quite often even established cultural agreements, trade relations, and profits from tourism have been sacrificed to political disputes. The effectiveness of these increases in social interaction on the amount of international solidarity and global good will remains to be demonstrated.

The single most prevalent means of attacking the problems of development in the Third World, that of foreign aid from the developed countries, is a good example of commitment to a means that may be not only ineffective but even at times counterproductive. Foreign-aid proponents argue that an influx of foreign aid will lead to development, which will lead to stability, which in turn will lead to responsible government and the security of the other powers of the world. But this argument is open to grave question. First, capital is only one of the necessary ingredients for development and by itself will not help much if other obstacles are not overcome; lack of technical skills and education, inadequate markets, inhospitable climate, poor health of the populations, and traditional religions and cultures are all obstacles at least as important as capital deficiency. Second, even if the foreign aid that is being given in the 1980s were adequate and relevant to the problems of development, there is no guarantee that this development would promote stability. It has often been the richer nations of the world that have started wars, not the poverty-stricken ones. And finally, within the society the process of development is usually destabilizing rather than stabilizing, at least in the short run. Small increases in welfare can cause sudden increases in the population, both among the very young by decreasing infant mortality and among the very old by increasing life expectancy. This added population in turn will create a great burden on the already deficient mechanisms of production and perhaps cause regression rather than progress. Tensions within the society may increase and erupt if a part of the population gains employment in the development industries and enjoys a much higher standard of living while most of the population remains at barely subsistence levels. Thus, foreign aid is by no means a panacea for the problems of underdevelopment; and just as the decentralized use of force contained the seeds of its own failure, this decentralized approach to the transfer of wealth in the international system does also.

We are not trying to argue by this example that foreign aid should be stopped because it is a disruptive rather than a calming force in international politics; rather, we are trying to point out the complexity involved in formulating and successfully implementing a policy that hopefully, in the long run, will improve the condition of humanity. More importantly, we are arguing that foreign aid is not by any means a process that will show immediate positive results, being in the short run perhaps very disruptive. Finally, we are noting that there are many international conflicts that do not have their roots in the kind of objective condition that foreign aid might remedy, but spring from a simple conflict of purpose. In such conflicts it is unlikely that the solution lies in the foreign-aid approach.

More recently, emphasis has switched from cooperation between rich and poor countries in areas such as foreign aid and investment to cooperation among Third World countries in an attempt to redefine the existing relationships between North and South. With the ever-growing realization that the inequality between rich and poor countries will only be exacerbated under rules of equality and reciprocity, such as the Most Favored Nation (MFN) clause of the General Agreement on Tariffs and Trade (GATT), the Third World countries have been demanding a new international economic order (NIEO). This movement, based on South–South lines of cooperation to deal with the North from a position of solidarity, takes a number of forms. International Commodity Agreements between producing and consuming countries in such primary products as sugar and coffee, in order to guarantee some stability in price and supply, are one example of this kind of cooperation. A more comprehensive attempt to build a new international economic order is embodied in the Lomé convention, named after the capital city of Togo, where it was signed. This agreement, between the European community and a group of African, Caribbean, and Pacific (ACP) countries, provided for a series of measures aimed at improving the lot of the poorer countries, including duty-free access to the European market for certain manufactured products from the ACP countries, stabilization agreements for a number of primary products, and access to capital from the European Development Fund (EDF).

The term *collective self-reliance* has come to be used to refer to efforts on the part of Third World countries to redefine more fundamentally the relationship between North and South. Organizations established by producing countries to offset the dominant role of consuming countries and Transnational Enterprises in some products, such as the Organization of Petroleum Exporting Countries (OPEC) and the less effective International Bauxite Association (IBA), are examples of this. Regional integration schemes with aspirations to fundamentally redefine relationships with developed countries, such as the Caribbean Community and Common Market (CARICOM), and steps toward development of Third World technology appropriate to local conditions and not subject to exorbitant payment to the patent holders through Technological Cooperation among Developing Countries (TCDC) are other examples of collective self-reliance.

The traditional diplomatic methods, the power approach, and the international cooperation approach to managing conflict and solving problems in global politics all depend upon individual acts of states in taking autonomous decisions to implement policies, generally without any centralized coordination or control. These are not the only means of resolving conflict, reducing violence, or increasing solidarity in international politics. There are other means; but rather than being mechanisms or forces that reside entirely within the foreign-policy discretion of the single state, they pervade the entire international system. Thus in a sense they are more centralized, and operate as international rather than national limitations on the anarchy of the international system. The most tenuous of all of these means is the appeal to morality. Closely related to morality is international law, which has been called by John Austin nothing more than public international morality. Finally, related to international law are international organizations created in order to provide institutions for the peaceful carrying out of international politics. We turn now to these international forces, procedures, and mechanisms.

Morality

In addition to political and economic factors, moral considerations also have some influence in international politics, usually but not always in the direction of counteracting the disruptive forces considered in Chapter 3. The moral teachings of the great religious and ethical systems unmistakably play a role in helping to influence the behavior of states and their leaders. The Ten Commandments; the Sermon on the Mount; the Golden Rule; prescriptions for honesty, tolerance, kindness, and generosity; codes forbidding deceit, theft, killing, and torture—these ethical norms and precepts play a role in international politics. Some of these teachings prompt states and their leaders to take certain actions; others are aimed at ruling out certain activities as immoral. To some extent these positive and negative moral injunctions are influential in determining political events; and the result of their influence is sometimes helpful.

Such moral factors can be brought to bear in international politics in essentially three ways. In the first place, the actions of individual statesmen are influenced by their moral and ethical values, their own consciences. There are some things they will want to try to do because their own sense of what is right will push them in that direction. Other acts may seem so personally repugnant on moral and ethical grounds that they will not countenance them. Moreover, their own set of values will inevitably shape their perceptions of problems and possible solutions and in this way strongly influence the actions they will take. Any situation may have facets that they will simply not see because of their ethical dispositions; and some responses will not even occur to them because their imaginations will be limited, partly by ethical preferences. Even today, when people attribute much that takes place in the world to the inexorable workings of fate or of social and economic forces, the perceptions and choices of individual leaders are still beyond doubt important factors in the history-making process; and these leaders are in turn strongly influenced by their values.

Second, moral factors can be brought to bear via domestic public opinion, the national conscience. All political leaders are influenced by the attitudes of their respective populations. Thus, they pay attention to public responses to their actions and attempt to anticipate public responses to contemplated future activities. In an open society with democratic institutions, the political leaders will naturally attempt to elicit widespread public support if only to gain or keep office. But even dictators will last only so long as their policies are generally acceptable to those who support them in power. No government, regardless of how strong, can govern without widespread voluntary compliance with its commands. Massive obstructionism and hostility will eventually bring it down—or fear of these will more likely cause the dictator's associates in the military and party hierarchies, who would like to keep their jobs, to oust their unpopular master. Moreover, political leaders everywhere, regardless of the nature of the regime, seem to have an exaggerated desire to be respected and loved—by everyone, if possible, but especially by the historians who evaluate their actions for posterity. So all political leaders are to a greater or lesser extent captives of their domestic publics.

The attitudes of their domestic publics are, in turn, in some degree a product of their ethical values. Public reaction to past and present actions—approval, indifference, uneasiness, condemnation—is partly a reflection of the public's moral assessment of the actions. And public pressure to take certain future actions but desist from taking others will be partly determined by the collective moral assessment made by the nation's citizenry and expressed in a variety of different ways. Besides being influenced by their own consciences, then, political leaders are also both prompted and restrained by the national conscience to behave in ways generally consistent with ethical norms.

The third channel through which moral factors influence statesmen is that of world public opinion, the collective conscience of humanity as it is sometimes called. Statesmen are unquestionably influenced by reaction or anticipated reaction from abroad to their words and deeds. Most leaders are sensitive and prudent enough to pay "a decent respect to the opinions of mankind" as they weigh their options. The statesman will, of course, pay more attention to some external reactions than to others; the views of an ally or long-time friend will usually be more influential than remonstrances by an unfriendly power, and strongly articulated opinions will be more influential than weakly felt views. The United States, for example, is likely to pay more careful attention to a view vigorously expressed by Her Majesty's Government in London than to a caustic rebuke from Bulgaria or a pious pronouncement from Tanzania, although even these are weighed. The risk of irritating or alienating other nations—large or small, friendly or not—is a risk statesmen would rather not run if they can adopt another option that reduces or avoids this particular risk. In a tense and divided world of easily irritated states, most seek inoffensive courses of action; thus, external public opinion, as well as domestic public opinion, will help shape foreign policies, prompting leaders to do certain things and discouraging them from doing others. The fact that statesmen pay attention to external public opinion is borne out by the elaborate lengths to which all governments go to justify their actions to the world; the "information" agencies, legal staffs, and speech writers of the world's states all have the important task of grinding out enormous quantities of propaganda designed to persuade ex-

ternal opinion that their respective regimes' actions are necessary, correct, wise, and just. Moreover, a key function of the
world's diplomats is to explain their governments' policies in
the best possible light, whether quietly at an informal luncheon
with other diplomats or dramatically in a formal United Nations
address. The large sums of money spent by all states, even the
poorest, to mollify world public opinion attest to the importance
governments attach to this important influence.

A certain part of this external opinion is morally based. To
some extent foreign peoples, statesmen, and governments react with approval or outrage or something in between because
of their moral attitudes toward the action or statement in
question.

Moral considerations brought to bear on foreign-policy making in any or all of these three ways are very often helpful in
contributing to the easing or solution of global tensions. Most
of the time most states conduct their relations with most other
states with an admirable adherence to such basic moral precepts
as honesty, tolerance, generosity, and friendship. We tend to be
blinded by daily examples of newsworthy outrageous behavior,
but we ought to realize that the bulk of international dealings
are ordinary and civilized, and thus unreported. The existence
of widely agreed-upon ethical codes of behavior is doubtless
instrumental in making international politics as trouble-free as
it is.

Moreover, more frequently than cynics would like to admit,
moral teachings are very influential in causing a state to take
some decent action or refrain from acting outrageously. One
reason for the foreign aid being sent to the Third World is
some sense of moral obligation the rich nations feel toward the
poor. One reason communist and predominantly democratic
nations seek to spread their respective creeds is a sincere feeling that the other people would benefit if they adopted the
suggested creed and its institutional concomitants. A major
reason the allied nations in World War II did not use gas warfare against the Germans and Japanese was the conviction held
by allied leaders that to do so would have been morally offen-
sive to them, morally unacceptable to their own citizens, and

morally outrageous in the eyes of the world. It was reported moral repugnance that deterred President John F. Kennedy from launching a surprise air strike ("sneak attack") to destroy the Russian missiles emplaced in Cuba in the autumn of 1962. So, moral considerations are certainly operative in ordinary day-to-day state behavior. And, even in more dramatic, significant, crisis situations, moral imperatives and restraints play an often crucial, sometimes decisive role.

However, it is painfully obvious that moral considerations cannot presently be depended upon to produce international order and justice. This sad fact is a product of the more fundamental fact that the world is divided into more than 150 sovereign states. And humanity's behavior is not governed as a whole by a single code of values to which all subscribe; rather each person's behavior is shaped by one of a number of the cultural-national codes that overlap at different places and occasionally differ sharply on fundamental questions.

Moralists have always recognized that the moral quality of an individual act is largely determined by two factors: first, the *context* in which the action takes place, and second, the *purpose* the action is designed to serve.

For example, despite general acceptance of the biblical commandment, the taking of a human life is considered morally acceptable by most people for some purposes in some contexts (as for self-defense) and unacceptable in others (as during an armed robbery), despite the commonality of the physical facts. In each of these hypothetical cases, person *A* kills person *B*; the fact that most would approve of the killing in one case but not in the other is entirely due to the differing circumstances. Only the most rigidly fanatical disciples of any code refuse to take into account the context and purpose of actions they are morally judging.

When statesmen take into account the fragmented world full of real and imagined dangers to their countries, they feel morally entitled to take certain actions they could not in good conscience take as private citizens. Indeed, they feel morally *obliged* by their solemn oaths of office to subordinate their own personal values to the statesman's supreme moral command: *Act so as to protect the nation.* Statesmen feel morally entitled, even obliged, to do whatever is necessary, within quite permissive limits, to maintain the safety of the nation, preserve the present form of government, and enhance the well-being of that nation's citizens. To execute the obligation they may lie, cheat, steal, be miserly and unkind, and even engage in large-scale killing to serve what they regard as a legitimate purpose within what they regard as a brutal context that legitimates such behavior.

When Franklin Roosevelt herded the West Coast Japanese into "relocation" camps during World War II, when Harry Truman authorized the use of the atom bomb in 1945, when Andrei Gromyko lied to John F. Kennedy about the missiles in Cuba in 1962, when a political leader has had his or her potential replacement assassinated, when the wealthy states have been stingy toward the poorer countries, the actions have always been explained as necessary to the national interest and hence morally justified; and the leader responsible is, by this reasoning, excused, even lauded for being morally courageous enough to make a difficult decision. Thus, at the present juncture, one very influential moral precept that finds almost universal acceptance cannot be depended upon to ease the world's problems and promote world order, because all too often statesmen will feel compelled to act otherwise. The supreme moral command that rules statesmen will frequently prompt them to contribute to strife rather than stability.

Most government leaders accept this characterization of the world and the extra moral obligation that they implicitly agree to hold supreme over their other values when they assume office. But even if a national leader were to waver or deviate from this commitment, either by inadvertence or conscious design, that leader would probably be either very quickly forced back into line or ousted by his or her ruling colleagues or domestic forces. For there is some truth to the suggestion that people force their leaders to adopt the hierarchy of values required of a statesman. We force our chosen leaders to subordinate all their previous values to the supreme value of protecting us and advancing the collective interest, even if to do so means that they must do things they would have thought reprehensible just before they took office. It is an onerous burden we impose, almost a cruel trick we play on leaders, expecting them to dirty their hands on our behalf. Most leaders, of course, know full well what they are getting into and energetically seek these burdensome jobs. The point here is that public opinion or the nation's conscience, which in some ways is a channel for moral influence in the foreign-policy-making process, cannot be any more depended upon as a force for order and stability than the statesman's conscience. Like the statesman's supreme moral command, domestic public opinion will insist that he or she do whatever is necessary for the nation's benefit, including acts that would be considered morally reprehensible by any standard of personal conduct. The world's various national consciences may help ease problems and promote order much of the time; but too often they contribute pressure in the opposite direction.

Nor is the conscience of humanity as a whole a very dependable ally in the search for order and justice. Humanity speaks with one voice only occasionally, and then only on quite settled and innocuous matters. More often in this divided and disorderly world, the statesman hears instead several dozen shrill and contradictory messages: some peoples and governments expressing approval, others outrage; some suggesting a particular policy, others demanding an exactly opposite course. And most of the disparate opinions expressed are not offered as much to promote order as they are to advance the speaker's national policy, which may or may not be designed to help the search for order. Thus, world public opinion so far is really little more than the usually disharmonious medley of assorted national opinions. As such, it remains of marginal value in conflict management or crisis resolution.

Finally, not only is there no single world value structure to guide and control the world's statesmen, but also, to make matters worse, the various value structures that do exist very often inhibit progress toward easing tensions, and even aggravate the world's difficult problems.

In many areas of the Third World, for instance, the prevailing creed is a principal obstacle impeding progress on the massive social, economic, cultural, and political problems that beset the area in question. Conservative, even reactionary, dogmas and values help perpetuate and even aggravate the stagnation and misery that we have seen are so explosive in the Third World. Only as these value systems are ignored, circumvented, or destroyed are the peoples of the Third World going to begin making progress toward a decent life. In the Third World, political decisions strictly based on the now-prevailing ethical values will clearly result in increased chaos. Moral teachings are not always the best guide to enlightened policy making.

Furthermore, value systems have a way of becoming full-fledged competing ideologies. The most dedicated followers of the ideology tend to become self-righteous, intolerant missionaries, anxious to spread Truth, Righteousness, and Salvation to the unfortunate and ignorant heathens. To the extent that this kind of person or this kind of ambitious and idealistic thinking controls the levers of state power, the state is apt to find itself zealously embarked on a moralistic crusade to the detriment not only of its own national interest but also of international order generally. It is probably historically true that more violence, injustice, and misery have been caused on behalf of the world's creeds by the self-righteous than on behalf of supposedly baser aims (like power or money or territory) by humanity's alleged villains. People who are eager to die for their ethical beliefs are dangerous people to have in public office. If moral teachings get thus twisted and then are taken so seriously that they imprison leaders and states, consequences inimical to world order can shortly ensue. This unfortunate state of affairs has occurred often enough in the past to prompt us to suggest that asking for moral considerations to be more influential in national policy making is a risky business at best. The line between moral behavior and self-righteous zeal is both dangerously fine and often crossed.

Moral considerations, then, are sometimes helpful in efforts to ease global tensions, although their effect is sharply limited by other' considerations. At other times moral teachings are unhelpful, counterproductive, even downright dangerous.

We turn next to international law, a method of conflict management which shares many of the uses and limitations that our brief examination of moral considerations has revealed.

International Law

International law is another factor in international relations that sometimes serves to mitigate the dangerous tensions we have discussed. Just as domestic law (or municipal law, as it is called by international lawyers) plays a role in allowing conflicts to be solved within the state, so international law has a similar role to play in the international system of politics. We can look to international law to provide certain rules of behavior which allow some international tensions to be solved without recourse to war.

Our discussion of the international system of politics in Chapter 2 indicated that the international system was decentralized, and that the institutional bases of order that we find in domestic society do not exist in a systematic, centralized fashion in international society. This difference does not mean that there is no such thing as international law, or that international law is completely ineffective in easing world tensions. To state it is simply to say that international law operates somewhat differently from municipal law. There is no international legislature, no international central police force to enforce the law, and only an imperfect international judiciary to settle conflicts under international law. International law does exist, however, and it does play a role in international politics.

When we say that international law exists, we are saying that there are rules of conduct directed at sovereign states, rules prescribing and proscribing certain modes of conducting relations with other states. The states of the world are aware of these rules and mutually recognize that they exist. The rules of international law cover a broad collection of activities and are considered to be universally binding on the states of the international system. Simply because the rules of international law are not generated out of an international legislative body and because they are not in a form similar to that of municipal law does not mean that international law is nonexistent. The sources and nature of international law are indeed different from the sources and nature of municipal law, but international law is no less real.

The sources of international law include international custom, bilateral treaties between two states and multilateral treaties between several, general principles of law found in civilized nations, previous rulings of tribunals adjudicating international disputes, the writings of scholars on international law, and certain rulings made by international organizations. The first two of these, international custom and international treaties, are the major sources of international law. The last four—general principles, previous decisions, the writings of legal scholars, and rulings by international organizations—play a lesser role in international lawmaking. The last of these sources is the most modern in origin.

Customary international law comprises rules which states have come to consider binding upon themselves and other states by virtue of their near universal usage over long periods of time. Freedom of the high seas is a prime example of customary international law. For reasons of convenience, expedience, or habit, states will begin to follow a particular pattern of behavior. After the passage of a certain period of time, most states will come to follow this custom because it is more convenient or safer to do so than not. Eventually, not only will this pattern of behavior come to be nearly universally followed, but it will come to be looked upon as the proper mode of behavior. When the states of the international system come to accept the customary pattern as obligatory, it becomes a customary rule of international law. The original reasons leading to the rule may have been forgotten, or have become irrelevant, but the rule stands as customary international law until it is replaced by a different custom or a formal treaty changing it. The fact that the law cannot be found in a code book does not make it any less law; and national and international courts alike will apply customary international law as binding on states.

With the rapid technological changes of modern times, international relations have expanded and become complex so rapidly as to relegate customary international law to a secondary role in international rule making. An international custom takes many years to mature into an effective international law; and this slow process is not adequate to provide modern international law for today's fast-moving world. For this reason, among others, the international agreement or treaty is assuming a more important position in the development of contemporary international law. The treaty is often compared to the contract in municipal law, a solemn agreement between two or more parties, in this case states, to respect certain rules as binding on the signatories.

Treaties are usually divided into two categories, bilateral treaties and multilateral treaties, the former being concluded between two states only, and the latter being concluded between three or more states. The bilateral treaty is somewhat limited in its lawmaking capacity, for it creates law binding only on the two signatory parties. Multilateral treaties, on the other hand, are binding in identical form on all the signatories, which in some cases include virtually all the states of international society.

The Charter of the United Nations provides a striking example of the power of a multilateral treaty. The Charter is itself a multilateral treaty, signed in 1945 by 51 states to create a global international organization. Since that time the number of states adhering to the principles of the charter by becoming members of the organization has grown to more than 150, making it one of the most widely adhered to multilateral treaties. This example of treaty making is particularly important because it involves the creation of a new international legal entity, the organization itself, through the lawmaking process of the multilateral treaty.

In some cases international law binding on all states of the international system can be created by a few states concluding a multilateral treaty with the intention of developing a general rule of international law. This principle is not one that is completely accepted in international law, but the undertakings of the states that are carrying out exploration of the Antarctic regions under certain multilateral treaty arrangements is an example where the rules agreed upon among the parties are considered to be binding on any other state that may wish to participate in these activities in the future. To do so, they must accept the rules already established. In outer space also, treaty-based law formulated by the few pioneers will likely apply to additional states as they undertake space exploration on their own. This situation does not seem to be too much different from the development of the law of the seas; maritime rules were developed as custom among the few early seagoing states. As more and more states took part in maritime commerce, they accepted the customary law of the seas without having taken part in the development of most of the rules. The multilateral treaty may become the modern counterpart of international custom in the development of general international law.

Springing out of the multilateral treaty is a modern source of international law that is playing a major role in creating law among states on a regional basis, particularly in Western Europe. The law created by international organizations presently plays only a small role in international politics, but it has the potential of assuming a much larger role as more highly developed international organizations are created. Presently the European Community, comprising the European Economic Community (Common Market), the European Coal and Steel Community (ECSC), and the European Atomic Energy Agency (Euratom), is the single major example of an international organization with the capacity to create international law that is, concededly, binding only on the member states of the community. The resolutions of the General Assembly of the United Nations are only of a recommendatory nature, and the decisions of the Security Council of the United Nations, although binding upon the entire international community, cannot be said to be international law, but only specific rulings designed to solve particular problems at hand. Organizations that are empowered to create binding law on their member states are called *supranational*.

Tertiary sources of international law include general principles, the writings of legal scholars, and the decisions previously rendered by courts. For the most part, these sources play only a minor role in international law; indeed, they owe their presence to the fact that international law is relatively poorly developed and often must rely on sources other than custom or treaty to find objective rules for resolving a conflict. Another factor relegating these sources to a third rank in international law is that none is universally accepted as a valid source of law in domestic legal systems. The Anglo–American common-law tradition has a much stronger base of previous decisions being determinative of the case at hand than does the codified law upon which European civil-law countries, for example, mainly rely. On the other hand, the European legal systems are much more likely to rely upon learned writings as an indication of law than are the common-law systems. But in international law the writings of legal scholars are usually only considered as evidence of the existence of a rule which has its basis in custom or treaty.

These sources of international law provide objective rules of behavior in the absence of centralized international legislative machinery, but they do not solve the problem of providing or finding an impartial judge to adjudicate disputes arising under international law. The international system, however, is not completely devoid of adjudicative machinery.

Both national courts and international courts provide the machinery to hear disputes under international law. Many cases of international law are in fact heard in national courts; the Supreme Court of the United States, as well as the high courts of other nations, has been the scene of many cases involving principles of international law. The capacity of national courts to provide adequate machinery to adjudicate matters of international law is quite limited, however, for two principal reasons. First, no state can be compelled to appear as a defendant before the courts of another state. Second, the national courts of a state are unlikely to be impartial in a case involving the state as a party to a dispute.

There are international tribunals, the most notable of which is the International Court of Justice, one of the principal organs of the United Nations. The decisions of this court are nominally binding, and it has a broad competence to hear disputes under international law. The major shortcoming, however, is that no state is obligated to submit a dispute in which it is involved to judicial settlement. A state cannot be forced to appear and have its case heard in court, although many states have signed an "optional clause" which gives this consent in advance. So the International Court of Justice has heard relatively few cases.

Some cases, of course, have been heard by the International Court of Justice, and many of the rulings handed down by this court have been eventually implemented by the parties involved. There is no guarantee, however, that the decision of the court will be honored. The problem of enforcement remains if either of the two parties chooses not to respect the decision of the court.

In addition to the International Court of Justice, there are other mechanisms for legal settlement of disputes, such as regional international courts, ad hoc arbitration bodies, and other quasi-judicial institutions through which international disputes may be adjudicated.

This discussion shows that much of the everyday orderly intercourse that takes place between states is regulated by rules of international law, most of which are generally respected. International relations would be much more anarchic were it not for these rules of international law. There are international norms of behavior that, although not created by a legislative body, do have the force of law. The areas in which these laws are least effective are the areas in which there is greatest political conflict, and thus most likelihood of recourse to war.

It is quite clear, therefore, that international law does not provide the remedy for all or even many of the tensions that we have discussed. The shortcomings should be at least partially evident from the foregoing discussion.

The lack of compulsory international adjudication and the lack of centralized enforcement are only two of the shortcomings. International law is a very loosely woven law with major gaps; there are important areas in which there is no clear, objective rule of law to govern behavior. Without custom or treaty to provide these rules, there will be no legal regulation. And even where there are rules, they are often not objectively discernible. There may be a major disagreement on exactly what the international rule prescribes, and thus limited legal capacity to regulate behavior.

The decentralized nature of international law means that sometimes international law is used to justify disruption rather than to help control it. By virtue of the degree of self-enforcement, the lack of an independent judiciary, and in some cases lack of specific rules, states can use international law to justify actions which may in fact undermine international peace. In the Vietnam War and in the Middle East conflict, for examples, both sides cited conflicting principles of international law to support the legality and justice of their positions.

Clearly, international law manifests serious shortcomings as compared to the relatively effective systems of municipal law within the more advanced sovereign states. The most serious shortcoming, however, is not in terms of the specific functions that law must perform in order to provide effective maintenance of order, but rather in the very consensual basis of the law itself. Any effective system of legal norms must rest on a basis of social solidarity and cultural homogeneity that permits a feeling of community to prevail. There must be a general willingness to agree on procedural principles and to abide by rules commonly formulated. At the present time the degree to which this community exists in the international society is minimal; until this community develops we cannot expect international law to assist much in resolving conflicts of vital interest among states.

In its present forms and at the present time, international law is not capable of providing decisive limitations upon the use of force in international politics, or of providing the means for relieving international tensions. The solution to these problems must lie elsewhere.

Although the primary focus of our discussion of international law has concerned the formal requirements of legislation, adjudication, enforcement, and the like, it is clear that there simply is not sufficient international consensus to permit international law to develop and function effectively.

In spite of this central and crucial shortcoming, significant advances in the establishment of formal institutions at the international level have been possible. These attempts to centralize and institutionalize conflict resolution in international politics are grouped under the heading "international organization."

International Organization

Although international organization in one form or another incorporates most of the other suggestions for managing conflicts and solving problems in international politics, it can be distinguished from all the rest by a single characteristic. International organization is an *institutional* approach to the establishment of peaceful international relations.

It has been observed that in the domestic political system political conflict is channeled through existing centralized institutions that contribute to the resolution of this conflict with minimal likelihood of resort to violence. International organization involves the attempt to establish in the international system effective institutions which will facilitate in a centralized fashion the task of peaceful resolution of political conflict. Although present-day scholars of international organization do not champion the naive view that violence can be eliminated from international politics simply by establishing the institutional machinery that is comparable to the organs of government of the sovereign state, this assumption held sway not too long ago. Today international organization is more properly regarded as a means of institutionalizing, and thus stabilizing, whatever practices and processes of peaceful conflict resolution have evolved, and to provide for an environment that will encourage their development. This is a rather broad statement, but it correctly describes international organization as a very broad approach to peace. Under the rubric of international organization can be found all the other approaches to conflict management or resolution.

First, international organization incorporates the force, or power, approach to limiting violence as represented in the balance-of-power or deterrence procedures in international politics. Examples of the force approach within international organizations would include attempts to establish an international police force, attempts to establish systems of collective security, and attempts to establish peacekeeping forces under the aegis of an international organization. Second, international law as a peaceful approach to international politics can clearly be seen in international organizations. The charter, the constitutional basis of an international organization, is a treaty itself, providing rules of international law. Third, international organizations have been established which provide for the impartial adjudication of international law by an international court, and, in the case of the European Community, for the actual legislation of international law in the form of international rule-making organizations. Fourth, elimination or reduction of international violence through the achievement of international solidarity and a feeling of common culture is represented in organizations that are designed to bring about international integration. Fifth, the international cooperation approach to peace is represented in the many specialized international economic, social, and cultural agencies which concern themselves with the nonpolitical aspects of everyday international life. Finally, international organizations provide useful centers where the world's diplomats can gather to discuss and negotiate.

International organizations may someday provide the institutional centers where the capacity to exercise violence in the name of the community would lie. In modern sovereign states the military and police forces exercise this centralized violence, and the establishment of a centralized international police or military force has been the subject of many treatises on international organization.

The League of Nations and its successor the United Nations are both examples of global international organizations that provide for the use of force, including military sanctions, in maintaining international peace and security. Yet neither of them established an international police force or standing army. The United Nations Charter, in Article 47, provides for a unified Military Staff Committee to coordinate the international force that was to have been made up of contingents of national armies used to enforce decisions of the Security Council. But the Article 47 scheme has never been implemented. The Security Council of the United Nations is assigned the primary responsibility for maintaining international peace and security. The Security Council possesses the authority to use force to maintain international tranquility. The provisions for the use of force, however, are not couched in terms of an international police force, whose purpose is to police all of international relations and to enforce international law. Rather, they are in the form of a collective-security arrangement. Collective security is characterized by Inis L. Claude, Jr., in his book *Power and International Relations* as an institutionalized form of the balance-of-power mechanism. As we have seen, the nineteenth-century balance-of-power system involved the constant shifting of alliances in order to counter any single state or coalition of states that threatened to dominate the entire system. The shifting alliances of the nineteenth-century system provided the mechanism through which major wars were prevented. World War I signaled the demise of this system, partially, it has been said, because the alliances had become rigid, with the unhappy result that two roughly equal opposing coalitions became enmeshed in a series of chain-reaction hostilities.

Collective security represents an attempt to provide a centralized, institutionalized form of the balance-of-power mechanism, which explicitly attempts to provide what the earlier balance-of-power system achieved in a decentralized manner. The United Nations Charter has formally outlawed aggressive war as a tool for foreign policy; and according to the provisions of the Charter, the Security Council can take enforcement action against any state judged by the Security Council to be an aggressor. The Security Council can impose sanctions ranging from verbal condemnation through economic sanctions to military operations against the offending power. The provisions of collective security bind all nations which are members of the United Nations to act together in a concerted effort to oppose, with force if necessary, any state which violates the provisions. As was the case with the balance-of-power mechanism, any state which violates the proscription against aggression risks defeat, because all the other states of the organization are bound to oppose the aggression. In theory, because the members of the United Nations have explicitly stated beforehand that they will concertedly oppose any aggressor, no rational decision will be taken to commit an act of aggression, because it would surely be unsuccessful. Thus, with these formal provisions for collective security in the Charter of the United Nations, peace should be maintained.

But the provisions for collective security in the United Nations were doomed to failure from the very beginning. There are several reasons for this, having to do with the very nature of the assumptions of collective security as much as with the era of the cold war in which the United Nations has operated. Hedging on their commitment to collective security from the very outset, the Charter's framers included the so-called veto of the great powers in the voting procedures of the Security Council. To act on substantive questions before the Security Council, the majority in favor of a motion has to include the United States, the Soviet Union, France, Great Britain, and China. Thus, no enforcement action can ever be taken against any of these five powers (or its allies) without its own consent, which it certainly will not give. The veto, however, is only a symptom of the nature of international politics during the cold war, and not itself a cause of disunity among the superpowers.

Disunity has been bred by the strong ideological overtones of the East–West conflict and the bipolar split that it represents. For any true system of collective security to operate, there must be a great deal of flexibility in the foreign policies of the several states, with any state being prepared to support a former enemy if a formerly friendly state has violated the provisions of the collective-security pact. If an ally of the United States, a Western representative democracy, were found to be guilty of endangering the peace, the United Nations, including the United States and her Western allies, would have to band together to oppose the offending state. The ideological and political divisions of the cold war make it impossible for such a collective-security system to operate effectively. The only occasion on which one of the major powers has acted in accordance with the principles of the United Nations and against its major allies was the Suez crisis of 1956, in which the United States and the Soviet Union jointly opposed the Franco–British–Israeli venture into Egypt. However, in this case true collective-security sanctions were not implemented because France and Great Britain backed down in the face of the opposition.

The Suez crisis serves to emphasize a further difficulty in implementing collective security in the cold-war period: the overwhelming preponderance of military power concentrated in the hands of the United States and the Soviet Union. Beyond the necessity for a general commitment to the maintenance of the system as a first priority, and the corollary necessity of each state's being willing to align itself with any other state to oppose the aggressor in spite of ideological concerns, collective security presupposes that power in the international system is distributed evenly among at least several powers. This kind of dispersion would assure that no state could expect to succeed in defeating the concerted force of all the other powers. Even if all requisites of collective security were fulfilled and the Security Council of the United Nations were able to act against either the United States or the Soviet Union, it would be impossible to muster enough force, even with all the other states of the international system, to confront the offending superpower with overwhelming military force. At best, an attempt to take collective-security action against one of the superpowers would risk large-scale thermonuclear war, far more destructive than a decision not to punish the aggressor.

The United Nations has not been able to provide an effective collective-security organization in the cold-war era; but conceding this fact does not mean that the United Nations has been totally ineffective in its attempt to institutionalize force in order to reduce violence in international politics. The rigidity of the cold war and the institutionalization of this deadlock in the Security Council veto has evoked the response of an evolution in the organization. The United Nations has shifted in its peace-keeping orientation toward grappling with the increasingly serious problems of the Third World. Most of the more than 100 members that have joined the organization since its founding are from the former colonial areas which make up the Third World and which take a neutral position in the cold-war conflict. Within the United Nations it has been the General Assembly, as the plenary organ in which all members are represented and have an equal vote, that has been the most profoundly affected. With the Security Council hobbled by the cold-war schism and the General Assembly greatly enlarged by members of the Third World, the focus of activity has shifted to the problems of maintaining peace through mechanisms other than collective security and in areas outside the main arena of the cold war.

The cases in which the Security Council has been able to come to agreement have either arisen under anomalous circumstances, such as the aggression of North Korea in 1950 when the Soviet representative was boycotting the Security Council, or else were not cold-war power confrontations, such as the defiance that led to sanctions against the racist regime of Rhodesia.

The result has been that instead of force being used in the name of the United Nations to combat aggression in the cold-war areas of the world, force has been used in an attempt to restore and maintain peace in areas outside the cold-war arena. And instead of the Security Council exercising primary responsibility for peace and security through the mechanism of collective security, this burden has shifted to other organs of the United Nations, namely the General Assembly and the Secretary General. Dag Hammarskjöld called this undertaking of the United Nations "preventive diplomacy," signifying that the role of the United Nations has shifted from one of maintaining peace among the antagonists of the cold war to one of attempting to prevent peripheral conflicts from becoming cold-war battle-grounds.

Thus the major use of force in the global international organization has involved military forces drawn from the smaller, nonaligned nations. In the Congo, the Middle East, and Cyprus, the Secretary General has been authorized by council or assembly resolutions to form military forces to restore and preserve peace without resort to use of the military forces of the major powers of the world. In this way, the United Nations has adapted itself to the constraints of the East–West dispute and, while not capable of guaranteeing peace in disputes involving the major powers, has been able to prevent the East-West schism from deepening every minor conflict that has arisen in the world.

Beyond simply institutionalizing a kind of balance of power to help maintain world peace, however, the United Nations operates in a much broader area of activity (see Figure 4.1). This global international organization has been designed to provide means for increasing the solidarity among the members of international society, which would enhance the ability to develop international law and would promote respect for international organizations. The Economic and Social Council, another of the six major organs of the United Nations, is specifically designed to alleviate economic and social problems throughout the world. It provides the instrumentality for channeling assistance in reducing the disparity between the rich nations and the poor nations; its activities are, thus, designed to help cope with Third World problems.

The Trusteeship Council is unique in that it is the one major organ of the United Nations that was designed to "work itself to death." Established for the sole purpose of supervising the eventual achievement of independence for the trust territories, it declined in importance during the 1960s and 1970s as virtually all of these territories achieved their independence. This organ was instrumental in demonstrating to the Third World that most of the developed nations were committed to the liquidation of colonialism.

The United Nations has also been active in opposition to the

Figure 4.1 The United Nations System.

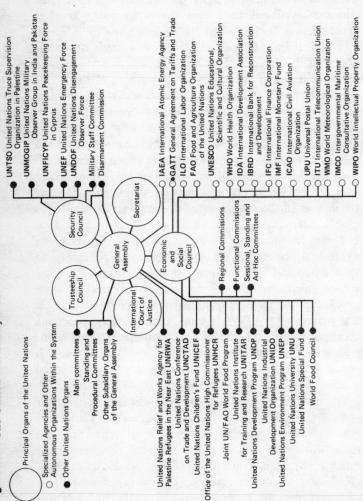

Source: (United Nations Office of Public Information.)

racist regimes of South Africa and Rhodesia (now the newly independent Zimbabwe), often at the behest of Third World countries. And it was a forum for pressure against Portugal, the last major colonial power which gave up its African colonies in the 1970s. These efforts are only a part of the general concern for human rights which the United Nations made a major focus, attempting to wrest this category of activity from the traditional "domestic jurisdiction" umbrella.

Through the organs of the United Nations, the wealthier states can provide economic aid to the underdeveloped states by transferring funds on the basis of technical considerations rather than political considerations, by technical assistance and education projects, and by special studies and reports prepared by the experts of the organization. The Economic Commission for Latin America, the Economic Commission for Africa, and the Economic Commission for the Far East are three examples of bodies that have been formed to study the special problems of these areas.

With the expansion of the membership of the United Nations to more than 150 states, mainly Third World countries, it was only natural for the organization to play a larger role in the North–South conflict. The regional economic commissions of the United Nations, particularly in Latin America through ECLA, but also in Africa, Asia and the Middle East, provided a stimulus to economic cooperation which fostered a number of regional economic integration schemes. The United Nations Conference on Trade and Development (UNCTAD) has become the principal institutional forum for efforts to create a more just international economic order. The United Nations Industrial Development Organization (UNIDO) has been the implementing agency for multilateral aid in industrialization and technical assistance projects. Over the past few decades the United Nations aid establishment has been dramatically expanded.

The task of increasing international solidarity is not limited to the underdeveloped areas or to the problems of the Third World. Associated with the United Nations through special agreements with the Economic and Social Council are many "specialized agencies," organizations that have specific, often technical tasks to perform that are crucial to the everyday life of individuals interacting across state boundaries. Examples of these are the International Labor Organization, the World Health Organization, the International Bank for Reconstruction and Development (commonly called the World Bank), and the World Meteorological Organization. These specialized agencies are examples of international organizations that institutionalize the cooperative approach to world peace.

The functionalists argue that international solidarity can be built through the establishment of a great number of specialized organizations which carry out the nonpolitical tasks of everyday international life, and that individuals will begin to cooperate in ever-broader areas of activity, whereupon nations will eventually forsake war as an instrument of foreign policy. Once it is discovered that benefits will be received through cooperation in these service agencies, and that joint action benefiting all is possible, there will be a greater willingness to endow the organizations with larger powers to undertake their activities. Eventually, cooperation will become so widespread that the participants in these organizations will all become too busy cooperating to fight, or will forget to fight, or will simply discover that the control of those institutions, resources, and activities necessary for warfare has shifted away from national governments to international organizations.

The United Nations is not the only international organization that represents the functional approach to world peace. In fact, the United Nations has been far surpassed in the degree to which it undertakes cooperation in broad nonpolitical areas of activity by the regional organizations in Western Europe. The specialized agencies of the United Nations represent a much less ambitious undertaking in functionalism than does the European Community.

In the 1950s, six countries of Western Europe (France, Germany, Italy, Belgium, the Netherlands, and Luxemburg) formed the European Community, thus undertaking history's boldest experiment in international organization. Expanded to nine members by the 1970s (the United Kingdom, Ireland, and

Denmark), the European Community was originally based on the principles of functional international organization but has gone far beyond simply increasing international intercourse to enhance the likelihood of peace. The European Community started with an attempt to give control of the vital industrial sectors of coal and steel to a common High Authority in order to avoid the possibility of the member states using this capacity to wage war on each other. This original plan, undertaken in 1950, has been broadened to include steps toward integrating the entire economies of the six states into a single economy, with the ultimate aim of achieving the integration of Europe on a political level. Through the vehicle of economic integration, the European Community aims to create a politically unified Europe, a community where intracommunity politics would take place through the peaceful institutionalized processes of an integrated society. It is an attempt to change the political relations of Western Europe from international politics to domestic politics.

It is unlikely that our generation will know whether the European experiment will ultimately be successful; but at the present time it is the most advanced example of attempting international integration through a regional functional international organization. It represents not only an attempt to approach the problem of effective international institutions through cooperation on mostly economic matters, but also an attempt to establish international organization on a regional rather than a global scale. While some people argue that international organization will be effective only if it is developed on a scale that includes the whole world, others argue that an organization is more likely to succeed if it is established on a limited basis, encompassing only states of a certain region of the world which already have many social, economic, and political concerns in common.

The regional approach to peace is represented by some other organizations that are less developed and generally less effective than the European Community. The Organization of American States is an example of a collective-security arrangement and a defense pact on the regional level for the western hemisphere.

The Arab League provides a basis for the coordination of foreign policies among states that share the Arab culture. The Organization for African Unity provides a basis for African states to deal with their common problems. The United Nations, a clearly global organization, contains specific provisions for the operation of such regional organizations.

The force approach to international organization, as represented in collective security or international police, has not been able to maintain peace in the post–World War II era, and the functionalist and integration approaches have yet to show that they can solve the problems of a fragmented world, either on a global or regional level. Even so, international organizations have provided ongoing centers of interaction, with permanent institutions where the states of the world are in constant contact with one another. They provide forums where states may publicly express their views of world affairs and their grievances, thus facilitating international communication. They provide a convenient means for contact and negotiation, as well as the opportunity of good offices, conciliation, mediation, arbitration, and even adjudication. Perhaps the main contribution of international organization has been to provide in a permanent form the institutional means for these traditional methods of diplomacy to operate.

Some General Problems

Diplomatic and power approaches have their limitations in preventing or managing conflict, economic and cultural techniques are only partially useful, moral teachings are quite imperfect, and international law and organizations are mechanisms whose capacities are clearly restricted. We have focused thus far on the uses and specific shortcomings of each of these regulatory mechanisms or procedures. But there are some general problems in getting them to work successfully to prevent or limit or end disorder; we will address ourselves to six of these general problems—in order: ignorance, neglect, parochialism, fit, timing, and scarcity.

The first of these general obstacles, or problems, is *ignorance*.

Too few people are sufficiently aware of the enormity and severity of the world's present problems. In part, this widespread ignorance is due to the fact that the world's educators—scholars and journalists—have not done their jobs as well as they should have.

Scholars have become so specialized that few of them survey and write of the world's problems with a sufficiently wide perspective. Valuing explanation more than prescription, and reflection more than action, most have not boldly attempted to influence events or policies. Valuing dispassionate analysis, they have not wanted to sound alarmist, and so have failed to communicate urgency. And scholars have usually looked down on direct communication with the masses; few scholars want the reputation of "popularizer."

For their part, journalists have been preoccupied with the day-to-day events; they are given little space by editors for analysis. Moreover, despite all their pretensions to independence, most newspapers, television networks, and journalists embody and reflect established perceptions and norms held by the governing and powerful groups in their respective host countries; such mass media are often not given to sharply critical assessments or urgent demands for national action. Unfortunately, the media too often tell the masses what the elites want them to hear, or what the masses themselves want to hear, or both.

In part, too, our ignorance is due to the fact that too few of the world's people are hearing or absorbing whatever realistic information is available. The others are too preoccupied with the often overwhelming task of securing life's basic necessities on a day-to-day basis in a harsh world, and thus have no time to worry about nuclear proliferation, Third World chaos, Kremlin intrigues, or environmental pollution. Or else they are illiterate, without schooling, even sometimes without awareness of the world beyond their villages. Or, even if they have the time and opportunity to fathom the world's urgent problems, they choose to avoid the unpleasant and discouraging activity of doing so. They may choose, instead, to remain ignorant of the world's depressing realities, either to maintain their mental stability or because they are convinced that in this age of specialization the world's problems are none of their business. Even if they decide to make an effort at comprehending, they may be virtually incapable of a nonnationalistic assessment, because they have been so effectively conditioned from the cradle onward by parents, schools, churches, mass media, youth organizations, and political parties. Most young adults have had their political views formed for years; and these views and values often distort all subsequent incoming information, blinding the individual to contemporary reality.

Finally, this ignorance is due in no small measure to the almost incomprehensible nature of enormous and complex problems. Who can understand the labyrinth of Soviet–United States relations? Who can tell India how to contain centrifugal tendencies? Who has an answer for, or even a partial understanding of, Middle East tensions? Who can comprehend the numbers that these problems entail: Three hundred million deaths in a thermonuclear war, a present world population of 4 billion people, a United States defense budget of hundreds of billions of dollars, a thermonuclear warhead with the power of 60 million tons of TNT—these numbers are virtually unintelligible. The mind boggles before these intellectual challenges. No wonder Einstein once remarked that "politics is much harder than physics." Ignorance regarding these problems is perhaps unavoidable.

Ignorance is, in turn, largely responsible for the second general problem, the problem of *neglect*. However useful the management procedures and mechanisms may be, they are not likely to be used if a danger is not perceived at all, or is not thought to be serious enough to merit response. Quite often, perhaps usually, people react only when a festering problem they had only dimly noticed becomes a dramatic crisis. Neglect and subsequent insufficient attention to a trouble spot can be caused by ignorance. Ignorance can and does breed inadvertent neglect.

But neglect is also a product of indifference. The willful neglect of recognized dangers is a further important reason why our imperfect collection of conflict-management devices is not called into use. Nations are often guilty of ignoring an inflammable situation because they unreasonably hope or wish it will go away, or because their leaders and peoples are indifferent to violence and suffering, or because they foolishly feel that a far-off problem does not and cannot affect them and is thus of no concern to them, or because they are unwilling to supply the personnel and money to support the use of one or another of the available, though imperfect, management procedures. Perhaps the best present example of a willfully neglected problem is the existence of biological agents of mass destruction that many states have stockpiled but failed to worry about controlling.

Awareness must procede concern, and concern must precede determination and commitment. Unfortunately, more often ignorance results in apathy, and apathy combines with indifference to produce neglect. The consequence is that the potentially helpful tools lie idle on the shelf.

Even the development of concern and determination, however, may not be enough because of the third general difficulty encountered in any effort to use these tools: the persistence of *parochialism*. In a divided world of many nation-states, all pursuing different and sometimes conflicting goals, there is an acute shortage of cooperation and common effort toward coping with those situations serious enough to have stimulated concern and commitment. The Americans and Russians have different ideas about how to keep nuclear weapons in check, while the French and Chinese disagree with both views. There are as many favorite solutions proudly advanced for dealing with the population explosion as there are governments to propose them. Each nation advances its own scheme for dealing with a given situation and then, clinging jealously to its sovereignty and independence, stubbornly resists overtures to modify or compromise or cooperate. This lack of community, this parochialism, inhibits the effective use of many conflict-management procedures, especially those that depend most on multilateral cooperation, such as international law, international organizations, and functionalism. We have already noted that each of these instrumentalities is limited by the diverse political nature of the present world. Here we do no more than reiterate this general problem of parochialism that plagues all the procedures and mechanisms designed to promote order in this divided world.

The fourth general difficulty in applying the available procedures is due to what might be called the problem of *fit*. Many of these procedures and mechanisms are simply inappropriate for dealing with what is usually a political deficiency, namely insufficient order. Military, economic, moral, legal, and organizational approaches are usually unsuited for preventing or dealing with power struggles, population cleavages, revolutionary fervor, and the like. Picking the right approach or the right mixture of approaches is a difficult task, which is quite often fumbled. Quite often states resort to military measures designed to promote order. The effort often fails and the result is more disorder and chaos than existed at the outset. The normally most appropriate approach for dealing with the political problem of disorder, that is, diplomatic procedures to reach political accords, is too infrequently used.

To some extent this problem of fit is due to the fact that military measures (and, to a lesser degree, economic tools) are more visible and dramatic than the slow, quiet workings of diplomacy. Statesmen can—they think—see and measure the results better. They think they are better able to determine whether or not progress is being made. Furthermore, military activities are more exciting and active; so there are always pressures for military action from those impatient to "get something done" rather than tolerate endless, tedious, unspectacular bargaining by diplomats.

Moreover, many nations spend a sizable part of their wealth on military hardware. Statesmen are understandably tempted to use their available military machines, in which they have invested so heavily. And the military leaders normally are quite influential in the decision-making machinery of their respective nations.

But perhaps the principal reasons for taking up the wrong tool are that the problem of disorder is not recognized as essentially a political problem and the job of promoting and maintaining order is not recognized as essentially a political job. Whatever order exists in any political system, whether within a nation-state or within the international system, is chiefly a product of a well-functioning political process that is effectively reconciling the interests of competing factions or states, producing justice and satisfaction, thereby ensuring widespread voluntary compliance, and thus promoting order generally. In such a smoothly functioning political system most issues are settled by bargaining—by deals, trades, compromises, and mutual back scratching. Only when the political system fails do the contestants go to court; out-of-court settlements are preferable to the rigid and embittering judgments apt to come from judicial proceedings. And, as all know, legal procedures are only the next-to-last resort; if both the political and legal processes break down, force and violence become the last resort.

Too often, however, domestic order is attributed to the state's legal machinery or to its coercive power, while the crucial importance of the political system is overlooked. High school students in the United States are told that their country is governed by the rule of law. They are perhaps also told that a nearby authoritarian regime rules with brute force and naked terror. In fact, both states owe their stability chiefly to general satisfaction with the political process and its bargaining outcomes, though in both states the ultimate sanction of coercive force resides with the state if needed.

It is easy to see how statesmen, and people in general, could move from this erroneous view of the source of domestic order to discount the political approach at the international level, as well. Failing to recognize the centrality of politics at the domestic level, they likewise fail to see that whatever international order we enjoy is due chiefly to the political bargaining carried out by political leaders and diplomats. The result of these failures is neglect of the diplomatic approach or merely half-hearted efforts to try it before moving on to other allegedly more productive techniques. And at the international level legal processes do not provide much of a next-to-last resort. Military force and violence are thus invoked as a remedy for disorder that often is politically rooted.

To note this tendency is not to say that the military approach will always be a bad "fit" or that many problems do not have an economic or technical or legal dimension. The problems of Third World disorder, for example, are clearly very complex and some sort of mixture of approaches will be required to cope with them or resolve them. But the essence of the problems is political. Disorder has its roots in an imperfect political system; order can be restored or maintained only under the aegis of a functioning political system. The Vietnam War is only one recent example of the impossibility of producing order by military activity within a country torn by civil war and lacking any real political system.

A fifth obstacle encountered in getting the conflict-management mechanisms to work effectively is the problem of *timing*. Most of the means we have analyzed are usually brought into use too late in an effort to cope with disorder that has already erupted. There is insufficient early use of any of them to prevent disorder. Too often these mechanisms, belatedly called in, are applied to symptoms instead of being constantly in use to deal with the root causes of disorder. And while several of these mechanisms can be quite helpful in the more positive and creative task of prevention by mitigating these root causes, most of them are ill suited for the more negative and reactive job of restoring order by repressing the symptoms. If conflict has boiled over into actual violence, it is usually too late for international law, moral imperatives, and economic incentives; it is often too late even to use diplomacy or international organizations very effectively. These tools are generally shelved for the duration, while the more coercive tools of police and military sanctions are taken up.

We have yet to understand fully that in the arena of international relations, as elsewhere, an ounce of prevention is preferable to a pound of cure. The truth of this old bromide is perhaps especially striking in international relations. Preventive medicine to eliminate or at least reduce the roots of strife is always cheaper than forcibly dealing with an outbreak of violence. Generally, too, prevention is easier because the ugly passions and intransigence of open conflict have not yet arisen to obstruct progress. Furthermore, prevention via economic, political, and other nonviolent approaches is inevitably less coercive and less destructive of the human spirit and human life itself than is repression of violence with police and military power. Finally, as has already been indicated, prevention is more feasibly a multipronged approach in which a variety of tools can be flexibly and creatively used as well as more adequately controlled by responsible authority; during disorder, on the other hand, fewer techniques are feasible and the approach is usually the less controllable, negative answer of countering violence with violence.

For all these reasons, it seems reasonable to suggest that the world's leaders ought to devote more energy and resources to the early identification of the roots of possible future strife and to the elimination or removal of these sources. International relations today, though, are still composed by and large of tardy employments of our imperfect collection of mechanisms and procedures for preventing or managing disorder, or both.

We have already alluded briefly to the sixth and final reason why the regulatory tools are not fully adequate for the job: the problem of *scarcity* of resources. Serious shortages of physical and human resources plague efforts to get these procedures functioning satisfactorily. Even if awareness and concern have replaced ignorance, even if determination has replaced neglect, even if a modicum of cooperation has partially displaced parochialism, and even if far-sighted statesmen are anxious to forestall strife rather than merely repress it, the struggle for order will falter if sufficient resources are not forthcoming.

Physical resources are obviously important. If East–West and Third World problems are to be effectively handled, organizations must be financed, equipment and land must be available, buildings must be built, food and raw materials must be secured, and military hardware must be stockpiled for the use of peacekeeping forces. Most of the management procedures we have analyzed in this chapter are to some extent dependent on expensive resources. Economic and military approaches are perhaps the most so, though international organizations and even diplomatic and legal procedures are often costly.

But human resources are perhaps even more critical and scarce. Our efforts to deal effectively with world problems falter because there are too few effective people—too few experienced bureaucrats, too few trained technicians and professionals, and, probably most unfortunately, too few wise and good government leaders. Land and money and machinery are scarce, true; but more importantly, such human qualities as judgment, talent, imagination, wisdom, knowledge, courage, magnanimity, vision, tolerance, and leadership are in unfortunately short supply.

There are, then, some general obstacles that impede the effectiveness of each of the conflict-management procedures or mechanisms whose uses and limitations we analyze separately in this chapter. We have itemized and discussed the problems of ignorance, neglect, parochialism, fit, timing, and scarcity that are very real and must be kept in mind.

The mechanisms for conflict resolution discussed in this chapter serve to demonstrate that international politics, while being much less centralized than domestic politics, is far from being completely without means to resolve conflicts peacefully. The means the international system possesses are diverse and incomplete and often are not entirely successful in diverting the outbreak of violence. Yet, when they are considered in the face of the international tensions that we discussed in the previous chapter, it can be seen that the task of managing international conflict is a difficult one.

SUGGESTED READINGS

Claude, Inis L., Jr. *Power and International Relations.* New York: Random House, 1962.

Claude, Inis L., Jr. *Swords into Plowshares.* 4th ed., New York: Random House, 1971.

Coplin, William. *The Functions of International Law.* Chicago: Rand McNally, 1966.

Nicolson, Harold G. *Diplomacy.* New York: Oxford University Press, 1964.

Walzer, Michael. *Just and Unjust Wars.* New York: Basic Books, 1977.

Chapter 5
The Struggle for Order

In the two previous chapters we have examined some important aspects of the struggle for order in the world. We have noted the principal sources of global tensions (Chapter 3), and we have analyzed the efficacy of some of the procedures and mechanisms presently available to deal with these tensions (Chapter 4). Now we need to combine these two analyses, evaluate the present status of the struggle, and try our hand at speculating about the future prospects for world order.

It should be clear by now—perhaps painfully so—that we regard these as perilous times. The world's problems are truly enormous and frustratingly complex; the obstacles to minimal world order are formidable, even frightening. Never before have we had the capacity to destroy humanity, either in a brief thermonuclear cataclysm or more slowly through environmental poisoning. Never before has overpopulation been such an ominous threat. Never before have so many newly created, fragile states been troubled by internal upheavals. Never before have human and physical resources been in such short supply relative to the tasks facing us.

Urgent as the problems are, efforts at creating ways to solve them and extricating ourselves from this ominous crisis have come to very little. We find ourselves equipped only with such weak tools as international law and organizations, diplomacy, and moral teachings, all of which are often misused by the world's states to serve unsound goals, with consequences that are often the opposite of what they were intended to provide. Quite regularly we find ourselves relying on force to counter force, with the unfortunate result that conflicts are expanded.

In sum, none of the regulatory mechanisms and procedures analyzed in Chapter 4 is really successfully dealing with, much less resolving, the crucial problems identified in Chapter 3.

The East–West conflict continues, heating or cooling from year to year as moral constraints, international law and organizations, cultural and economic approaches, and even diplomatic and power procedures prove unable to end it. The two superpowers continue mutually fearful and hostile. Europe continues divided. The tragic and dangerous arms race continues with a momentum of its own. And well-meaning efforts to bring would-be regulatory mechanisms to bear have come to little more than an occasional conference that reaches a usually marginal accord that may or may not endure. The collection of instrumentalities in our pitiful arsenal of order has not given us much help in defusing this critical East–West confrontation.

These instrumentalities have been no more helpful in resolving or even easing the Third World's dilemmas than they have been in ending the East–West dispute. Again, the problems have overwhelmed the regulatory devices available for assistance. Economic and technical aid have had a negligible effect on poverty and population pressures; in fact, the aid is often such that it exacerbates the problems by stimulating medical advances that promote population growth. International organizations have sometimes played a useful role in easing the transition from colonial rule to national independence, as in the case of United Nations intervention in the Congo in the early 1960s, but for the most part international organizations have played a very small part in limiting Third World strife. International law and moral considerations have, as in other areas, been more useful as postdecisional rationalizations for often destabilizing state policies than they have as aids in forestalling or containing international or internal violence in the Third World. The same is true of military and diplomatic techniques; these have chiefly served not-always-harmonious state purposes rather than the general goal of order. The Africans and Asians have proved as adept as the European Machiavellians at using all these approaches as national-policy tools first and conflict-management aids second.

Likewise, these approaches have not yet really been very helpful in addressing the more recently perceived problem of environmental deterioration, the third of the great threats to global order—even species survival—that we discussed briefly in Chapter 3. Military might is of no use here, is even, in fact, part of the problem as the world's military machines voraciously consume scarce resources. Similarly, economic approaches more often than not contribute to environmental problems, because the favored technology and industrial projects in poor Third World lands result in pollution and resource depletion. Moral codes are no more helpful, because most are *homocentric,* that is, they appear to license and even encourage the domination and continued misuse of nature by man. So far diplomacy and international law have made minimal contributions to the task of saving and properly using humanity's life-supporting biosphere.

The present, then, can be accurately characterized only in somber, even alarmist, tones. Awesome problems abound, and ways have yet to be found for grappling successfully with them.

A Bleak Future?

What of the future? Is it only realistic to despair? Is it impossible to be hopeful? Generally, we would answer that the future is sufficiently bleak that optimism seems unwarranted, but not so totally hopeless that defeatism is justified. As we peer into the future, we can appropriately feel deep concern; yet there are a few bright spots in an otherwise grim picture.

The clearest and most disturbing characteristic of the future will probably be the continuation of strife and even repeated armed violence. The present problems are not going to disappear in the foreseeable future. East–West tensions and Third World instability promise to continue for some time to come, perhaps indefinitely, though some periods may be less dangerous and violent than others, and some improvements may be possible. Moreover, the underlying sources of these problems seem destined to continue: fear, mistrust, ideological fervor, arms races, injustices, misery, the population explosion, and their likes. None of these disturbing sources of tensions seems to be diminishing in strength and influence very much. Perhaps all of these sources can, in turn, be attributed to relatively unchangeable and flawed human nature. We seem unable to overcome our antisocial and violent impulses to match our rapidly developing capacity for destruction. Neither are we very good at learning from our prior misfortunes, or at developing our political and social skills in pace with our amazing technical competence. It seems highly likely, then, that the world will continue to be a tense and often strife-torn spaceship.

Indeed, the tensions will probably increase as they continue. They show no signs of being finally resolved or of mysteriously disappearing, and only threaten to become more complex and more serious as time goes on.

In the first place, tension grows because the major states of the world are increasing their nuclear destructive capacity daily. Each of the two superpowers has for years had the capacity to destroy humanity and all its creations (as well as most planetary life) several times over. Every year new technical refinements make our enormously destructive weapons more destructive and their delivery more accurate, while reliance on them inevitably makes it more difficult to control or eliminate them. The optimum time for international control of nuclear energy has certainly escaped us; each day we move beyond that time, disarmament or significant arms control is that much more difficult. Furthermore, those interested in nuclear arms control now have to consider several other nuclear states besides the United States and the Soviet Union: France, Great Britain, India, China, perhaps Israel; and perhaps, by the mid-1980s, Pakistan, South Africa, Brazil, Japan, Iran, and others with the technical and financial capability, as well as with persuasive political incentives, to join the prestigious nuclear club.

In many quarters it is viewed as remarkable that the world has not suffered nuclear war in the years since World War II. If this happy fact is surprising, can we really expect to avert nuclear war indefinitely, or even for the rest of the century, now that we have more weapons that are more powerful in the hands of more states with conflicting goals? If it is remarkable that five or six or seven nuclear states have been able to balance uneasily on the nuclear tightrope for a few years, what hope can we really have if another dozen less experienced and more excitable acrobats join them?

The psychological anxiety resulting from "living with the bomb" is a second reason for suggesting that the future may be even more tense than the present. Profound anxiety may lead to irrational actions taken in panic situations by understandably nervous people. Or it may promote paralysis, based partly on fears that any action may be destabilizing and partly on fatalistic conviction that any action will be futile. In either case, world order will suffer as people lose, or think they have lost, the ability to control their destinies. Doubts about whether people are still in command of the human condition are already widespread. If we have in fact lost control, or, almost as important, if we think we have lost control over these powerful forces, our future is indeed bleak.

A third reason for expecting more tension can be found by looking to the underdeveloped world; there we can conclude only that most of the situations are going to get worse before they get better. Population in most areas is increasing faster than industrial and food-growing capacity, resulting in more and more people struggling to subsist on less food, fewer goods, and overburdened services. Internal conditions seem to be worsening as the anticolonial cement that united disparate factions crumbles, and as successive governments are unable to establish their claims to allegiance by satisfactory perform-ance in response to greatly increased demands. The Third World is already seething and occasionally erupting. Unfortu-nately, the future seems to hold more of the same.

Fourth, it seems likely, too, that things will get worse on the environmental front in the years just ahead. The human popu-lation will grow from 4 to over 6 billion people in the next 20 years, straining the earth's carrying capacity perhaps beyond its limits as this burgeoning population will need food, clean water, fresh air, firewood, oil, metals, and building materials. They will almost certainly also contribute further to the pollu-tion of this fragile environment by burning fuel to dirty the air and dumping waste products to foul land and sea; this polluting will accelerate with the spread of industry and mechanized agriculture.

Most of the weaknesses that limit or even cripple our conflict-management mechanisms and procedures will also probably continue. None of the approaches we analyzed in Chapter 4 is apt to be so strengthened during the next few decades that it will become a substantially more reliable instrument in the search for order. States will continue to be the dominant inter-national actors. And these states will continue to use (and misuse) their power, alliances, diplomats, wealth, and value structures in support of goals that will sometimes sharply collide with the goals of neighboring states. International law will likewise remain ambivalent—at best an occasionally useful conflict-management instrument, at worst a source for policy rationalization by even the most cynical and dangerous states-men. International organizations will continue to be weak because states will refrain from turning over their decision-making powers and their destinies to supranational government-like bodies. Decentralization and diversity will continue to characterize the international system for the foreseeable future, in spite of the often-made claim that the state is obsolete because it has lost its ability to protect its citizens.

The general obstacles to world order that we identified at the conclusion of Chapter 4 will probably remain. Ignorance, neglect, parochialism, indifference, and other human shortcomings will almost certainly persist for the foreseeable future. Human nature changes only very slowly, if at all. It would be surprising if these ancient traits were to change much in the next few decades. Human beings promise to persist in their foolishness, incompetence, and evil; and the institutions people build will continue to reflect the characters of the people who build them.

The outlook for the future, then, is not promising. Optimists have a very difficult time supporting their faith in a future of any sort for humanity, much less a pleasant, orderly future. Quite often, of course, optimists merely duck the grim facts and look the other way in the dangerous hope that those grim facts will vanish. Or, optimists depend on technology to solve these awesome challenges, much as it has solved such simpler tasks as making airplanes and tall buildings—without realizing that technology is adding to our problems, as well as sometimes helping to cope with them. Or, optimists naively count on some mysterious balancing process, some automatic "invisible hand," to prevent humanity's self-destruction; this naive assumption of some kind of automatic equilibrium is dangerous to the extent that it encourages inaction and overreliance on the protective watchfulness of the gods. Such ostrichlike behavior or naive faith is not going to do the job of preserving the human species; we think it quite clear that great efforts by concerned, skillful, compassionate people will be necessary during the coming years.

That such efforts will in fact occur may be doubted. Awareness and concern do not seem about to replace ignorance and indifference; yet these must precede commitment, cooperation, and reallocation of scarce resources if any struggle to escape humanity's dangerous dilemmas is to have even a fighting chance.

A Cautious Hope?

But perhaps there are a few promising signs, a few bright spots in this picture, a few small reasons for cautious hope. In the first place, a degree of awareness does seem to be developing, which is first and foremost an awareness of the dangers involved if we merely continue along the same courses we are presently following. Thoughtful people, both within and outside the governments of the world, are increasingly sensitive to the folly of continuing political "business as usual." They are apparently increasingly, if slowly, coming to realize that a world armed with destructive power sufficient to destroy us all can no longer afford the traditional forms of international behavior. Major-power warfare is increasingly recognized as no longer the rational instrument of foreign policy that it once may have been. A growing fear of what a nuclear holocaust would mean for humanity has induced a degree of moderation and prudence. In a very real sense a kind of global community of fear has emerged, as most of the government leaders and thoughtful private citizens of the world have increasingly come to realize that people must learn to live with each other, however grudgingly, if we are to survive at all. Being reciprocally menaced by nuclear weapons tends to force us together very much like the emergence of an external threat unifies squabbling domestic factions within a nation at war. The wary coming together is almost what we might expect humanity's reaction would be to a threat from outer space: the submerging of quarrels that would no longer seem so important, unity in the face of adversity, coordinated defense, and imposed cooperation.

To be sure, this rather negative community of fear does not mean that we have left behind all our differences or that we will do so in the foreseeable future. What it does mean, however, is that perceptive and rational people are increasingly coming to recognize that we all have a common interest in survival in a world which demands that we subordinate our differences to this common interest. Never before have leaders and citizens alike had to worry so much about the possible demise of humanity. There are encouraging signs that government leaders are increasingly keeping this feared consequence in mind when they weigh their options; and to the extent that they are thus apprehensive, their ambitions are more moderate and their actions more cautious.

These signs can be seen in events involving the conflict between East and West and the problems of the Third World. The United States and the Soviet Union have undertaken the high-level Strategic Arms Limitation Talks (SALT) with the aim of reducing the danger of nuclear war. In the area of space exploration the United States and the Soviet Union have become aware of the need for mutual and cooperative efforts as people are sent pioneering into the hostile environment of the moon, and beyond. Common efforts to develop safety and rescue operations have become the basis of joint endeavors. In Western Europe, West German leaders have visited the Soviet Union and important steps have been taken to normalize the relations between East and West in this central area.

There has also been a growing awareness of the problems of poverty and hunger of the Third World. The minds of some of our best scientists have been directed toward the development of "miracle" strains of rice and wheat, in order to permit the production of unheard-of amounts of food from previously marginal land. Nobel Peace Prizes in recent years have gone to the Food and Agriculture Organization (FAO) of the United Nations, the United Nations International Children's Emergency Fund (UNICEF), and an American scientist who developed a "miracle" strain of wheat.

There seems also to be a growing conviction, at least in the developed countries, that narrow nationalism is dangerously inappropriate in a shrinking and explosive world. More and more thoughtful people, perhaps especially in the Western world's younger generation, are becoming convinced that all the world's peoples are in the same leaky boat, for better or worse, and that if we are to survive at all we have to put aside our intolerant national creeds and abandon our instant readiness to do battle on behalf of abstract principles or vague notions about national honor. We have to begin thinking of humanity, rather than the nation, as the group, and of the international system rather than the sovereign state as the fundamental political structure to improve and strengthen so it can provide the requisite order and security. We have to replace nationalistic patriotism with what John Herz calls an attitude of universalism. To the extent that these sentiments become widespread, we can expect that romantic crusading and ideological confrontations will decline. And we can also expect a correspondingly increased commitment to solve humanity's manifold miseries—an increased generosity toward newly adopted brothers. Granted, these universal sentiments are painfully slow in developing and seem not to be emerging at all in some parts of the world; nonetheless, their gradual emergence in at least some quarters may be interpreted as a small, hopeful sign.

As we argued in the section of Chapter 3 on the endangered global environment, there seems, too, to be a dawning awareness of the fragility of the biosphere, the limits to growth, the dangers of resource depletion and biosphere pollution. Some even seem to be groping toward a new ethic: less homocentric and reckless; more sensitive to humanity's place in the natural, biological order; more genuinely conservationist.

A final sort of awareness that seems to be encouragingly, if slowly, developing is awareness that conflict prevention is preferable to conflict management or conflict suppression, and that early efforts to remove root causes of strife with economic, social, and political approaches are more effective and more desirable in many ways than tardy, usually military, efforts to resolve conflicts once they have erupted. The world's leaders and thoughtful citizens are slowly comprehending the costs, the risks, and the limits of military techniques for repressing disorder, and seem to be more inclined to spend the inevitably lesser amounts of energy and resources required for forestalling disorder in the first place.

Perhaps the major powers, especially, are learning that the possession and even application of military power is often of little use to the state interested in influencing world events and preventing or managing conflict. Both the United States and the Soviet Union are increasingly aware that they are, in a sense, muscle-bound giants unable to use their awesome physical power very effectively on problems that require a watchmaker's touch and a psychologist's intuition.

There are some hopeful though obscure hints that these superpowers, as well as other states, are determined to develop the subtlety, flexibility, and diverse skills for dealing imaginatively with the causes of conflicts, rather than merely dealing clumsily with their symptoms. More and more, scholars and leaders are attempting to understand the complex roots of violence and trying to develop a multipronged effort to come to grips with these underlying causes. Multilateral approaches with economic, cultural, and political tools are being formulated more often and are even getting the requisite financial support. Multifaceted efforts to promote tolerant coexistence and even cooperative coordination in U.S.–USSR relations have to some degree replaced the earlier, largely military, confrontations in the relations between these two great states. And finally, in recent years there has been a noticeable attempt to improve diplomatic procedures for forestalling or resolving the world's tense situations; this welcome turn away from propagandistic conference diplomacy toward productive quiet diplomacy promises to continue, and will aid our efforts to identify and deal with potential troubles before they erupt into open violence.

We can take some comfort, then, in situationally imposed moderation and the limited hints that some people, at least, are becoming more rational, as well as more compassionate.

We can also derive some comfort from the momentum toward moderation, rationality, and compassion that has already developed. Hopeful precedents and habits have been established and will be influential in shaping future events. Moderate, rational, and compassionate programs have been launched and will probably be expanded and built upon rather than scrapped; few things are as hard to abandon as a popular government program once begun. Social, political, and economic organizations to bind the world together and grapple with its problems, like the United Nations and the World Bank, are in existence and will probably increase the scope and effectiveness of their activities. Appealing ideas, like coexistence and universalism, will most probably be impossible to squelch. Each of these developments—programmatic, institutional, philosophical—already displays enough momentum to enable us to conclude that it is a most welcome and encouraging indicator of things to come in a world where encouragement is hard to come by.

Besides growing awareness and developing momentum, a third encouraging development is our improving capability for backing up our efforts to deal with disorder and violence. The knowledge and technical skills we have developed over the past few years will, if properly directed, assist our attempts to prevent or curb disorder. Significant progress in the areas of population control and food production is quite possible in the near future. Extracting food, raw materials, and fresh water for irrigation from the oceans may soon be practicable and economical. Great improvement in Third World government performance, legitimacy, and thus stability is conceivable if our constantly improving knowledge about communications and public administration is well applied by increasingly more able officials in the poorer countries. The fact that many of the developed countries now enjoy economies of abundance rather than of scarcity means that these developed countries will be better able to assist the Third World toward stability, especially if arms budgets in developed countries level off or decline as they safely could. In short, there is reason to suggest that the know-how and the wherewithal are rapidly improving to the point where they could provide impressive backing if the commitment to grapple ambitiously with the world's problems develops.

So the future is not unrelievedly bleak; there are a few hopeful signs that, if we act wisely, energetically, and soon, we may yet avert the catastrophe otherwise in store for us. The world is presently a most dangerous place and many signs indicate that the dangers will increase, perhaps even get out of hand, in the decades ahead; the human condition now is grim and the human race may not have much of a future. But we may yet prevail if the few hopeful tendencies we have identified are energetically encouraged by wise leaders who are encouraged or forced by a concerned, determined, and sensible global citizenry. It is probably naive to be optimistic; but perhaps it is at least possible for one to be cautiously hopeful—to be, as John F. Kennedy once described himself, an "idealist without illusions."

SUGGESTED READINGS

Boulding, Kenneth. *The Meaning of the Twentieth Century.* New York: Harper & Row, 1964.

Fromm, Erich. *May Man Prevail?* New York: Doubleday, 1961.

Marx, Leo. *Machine in the Garden.* London: Oxford University Press, 1964.

Schumacher, E. F. *Small Is Beautiful.* New York: Harper & Row, 1973.

Index